SAINT MARTIN
SAINT BARTS

3rd edition

Pascale Couture

ULYSSES
TRAVEL PUBLICATIONS
Travel better... enjoy more

Author Pascale Couture	**Production Supervisor** Pascale Couture	**Series Director** Claude Morneau
Project Supervisor Claude Morneau *Assistant* Stéphane G. Marceau	**Layout** Stephanie Heidenreich **Cartography** Patrick Thivierge Yanik Landreville	**Photography** *Cover Photo* Mark Bolster (Réflexion) *Interior Photos* Claude Hervé-Bazin Lorette Pierson
Translation Danielle Gauthier	**Illustrations** Lorette Pierson Marie-Annick Viatour	**Design** Patrick Farei (Atoll)
Proofreading Stephanie Heidenreich		

Thanks to Benoit Prieur and Stéphanie Couture, Mmes Élise Magras (Saint Barts Tourist Office), Rollina Bridgewater and Maryse Romney (Saint Martin Tourist Office).

DISTRIBUTORS

AUSTRALIA: Little Hills Press, 11/37-43 Alexander St., Crows Nest NSW 2065, ☎ (612) 437-6995, Fax: (612) 438-5762

BELGIUM AND LUXEMBOURG: Vander, Vrijwilligerlaan 321, B-1150 Brussel, ☎ (02) 762 98 04, Fax: (02) 762 06 62

CANADA: Ulysses Books & Maps, 4176 Saint-Denis, Montréal, Québec, H2W 2M5, ☎ (514) 843-9882, ext.2232, 800-748-9171, Fax: 514-843-9448, www.ulysses.ca

GERMANY AND AUSTRIA: Brettschneider, Fernreisebedarf, Feldfirchner Strasse 2, D-85551 Heimstetten, München, ☎ 89-99 02 03 30, Fax: 89-99 02 03 31, E-mail: Brettschneider_Fernreisebedarf@t-online.de

GREAT BRITAIN AND IRELAND: World Leisure Marketing, Unit 11, Newmarket Court, Newmarket Drive, Derby DE24 8NW, ☎ 1 332 57 37 37, Fax: 1 332 57 33 99, E-mail: office@wlmsales.co.uk

ITALY: Centro Cartografico del Riccio, Via di Soffiano 164/A, 50143 Firenze, ☎ (055) 71 33 33, Fax: (055) 71 63 50

NETHERLANDS: Nilsson & Lamm, Pampuslaan 212-214, 1380 AD Weesp (NL), ☎ 0294-494949, Fax: 0294-494455, E-mail: nilam@euronet.nl

PORTUGAL: Dinapress, Lg. Dr. Antonio de Sousa de Macedo, 2, Lisboa 1200, ☎ (1) 395 52 70, Fax: (1) 395 03 90

SCANDINAVIA: Scanvik, Esplanaden 8B, 1263 Copenhagen K, DK, ☎ (45) 33.12.77.66, Fax: (45) 33.91.28.82

SPAIN: Altaïr, Balmes 69, E-08007 Barcelona, ☎ 454 29 66, Fax: 451 25 59, altair@globalcom.es

SWITZERLAND: OLF, P.O. Box 1061, CH-1701 Fribourg, ☎ (026) 467.51.11, Fax: (026) 467.54.66

U.S.A.: The Globe Pequot Press, 6 Business Park Road, P.O. Box 833, Old Saybrook, CT 06475, ☎ 1-800-243-0495, Fax: 800-820-2329, sales@globe-pequot.com

Other countries, contact Ulysses Books & Maps (Montréal), Fax: (514) 843-9448

*I hope that succeeding generations
will be able to be idle... that they may
rest by the sea and dream...*

The Story of My Heart
Richard Jefferies

TABLE OF CONTENTS

SYMBOLS

🦎	Ulysses' favourite
☎	Telephone number
⊠	Fax number
≡	Air conditioning
⊗	Ceiling fan
≈	Pool
ℜ	Restaurant
⊛	Whirlpool
ℝ	Refrigerator
K	Kitchenette
△	Sauna
⊖	Exercise room
tv	Television
bkfst	Breakfast

ATTRACTION CLASSIFICATION

★	Interesting
★★	Worth a visit
★★★	Not to be missed

HOTEL CLASSIFICATION

Prices in the guide are for one room, double occupancy in high season, unless otherwise indicated.

RESTAURANT CLASSIFICATION

$	under 60 F
$$	60 F to 125 F
$$$	125 F to 200 F
$$$$	over 200 F

$	under US$10
$$	US$10 to US$20
$$$	US$20 to US$30
$$$$	over US$30

The prices in the guide are for a meal for one person, not including drinks and tip, unless otherwise indicated.

LIST OF MAPS

MAP SYMBOLS

❶	Tourist Information	🏰	Fortress
✈	Airport	▲	Mountain
🚌	Bus Terminal	◎	Beach
🚗	Ferry	✉	Post Office
Ⓗ	Hospital	✝	Church

"We acknowledge the financial support of the Government of Canada through the Book Publishing Industry Development Program (BPIDP) for our publishing activities." We would also like to thank SODEC for their financial support.

WRITE TO US

CATALOGUING

Canadian Cataloguing in Publication Data

Couture, Pascale, 1966-

   Saint-Martin, Saint-Barts

   3rd ed.
   (Ulysses due south)
   Translation of: Saint-Martin, Saint-Barthélemy.
   Previously published as: Saint Martin, Sint Maarten, c1996;
   and as Saint Barts, c1996.
   Includes index.

   ISBN 2-89464-212-1

   1. Saint-Barthélemy - Guidebooks. 2. Saint-Martin
(Guadeloupe) - Guidebooks. I. Title. II. Series.

F2103.C6813 1999   917.297,604   C99-940863-1

 Where are Saint Martin and Saint Barts ?

Island of Saint Martin	Island of Saint Barts
Territory divided between France and the Netherlands	Overseas French department
Main cities: Phillipsburg and Marigot **Languages:** French, English, Dutch and Creole **Population:** 69 000 inhab.	**Main city:** Gustavia **Language:** French **Population:** 6 500 inhab.

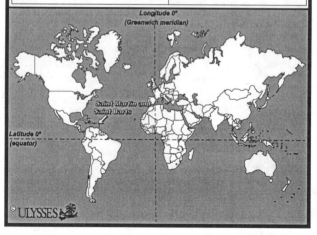

PORTRAIT

O rient Bay, Long Bay, Oyster Pond, Anse de Grande Saline... so many beaches conjuring up dazzling sunshine beaming down on azure waves, fine sand caressing feet, waves gently lapping the shore, the sea breeze... a symphony for the senses inviting pleasurable idleness.

Saint Martin and Saint Barts, the two islets at the northern tip of the Lesser Antilles archipelago, have been popular destinations at various points in history. Arawak-speaking aboriginals were undoubtedly the first to settle here over 3,500 years ago. These people – the only ones to have lived on this peaceful land for centuries – were later followed by successive waves of immigrants from South America. The next to land on these islands were the Europeans who, in the space of less than two centuries, became their sole rulers. French and Dutch colonists gradually settled there, but, far from finding the abundance they had hoped for, found themselves cultivating a barren land. For decades, nature proved a dauntless foe; intense sun and hurricanes were the cause of much hardship. Having slowly abandoned hope of cultivating anything here whatsoever, residents had to wait until the beginning of the 1980s before managing to derive any benefit from nature. This barren, untamed land nevertheless boasts idyllic beaches and shimmering waves that draw thousands of visitors every year.

GEOGRAPHY

Composed of over a hundred islets set in the sea like a long string of pearls, the archipelago of the Lesser Antilles was formed several million years ago by the movement of tectonic plates. In fact, an upsurge of magma had then driven the Atlantic plate toward the coast of the Americas. This plate, embedding itself beneath the smaller Caribbean plate, caused a host of little islands to emerge: the Lesser Antilles.

Lying at the northern extremity of this archipelago, Saint Martin is an arid island. Hillsides rising from the centre of this island are covered in sparse vegetation, comprised of shrubs and cacti. Its landscape is also distinguished by long crescent-shaped beaches punctuated by a few lianas and sea-grape trees, as well as great salt-water ponds (Simson Bay Lagoon, Great Salt Pond). These salt marshes, which have been exploited since the onset of colonization, were formed as sediment was deposited at the mouth of torrential rivers (in which the volume of sediment is particularly high during cyclonic floods), thus creating long coastal ribbons of sand and closing off large lagoons.

Barely 30 kilometres south of Saint Martin, Saint Barts emerges from the waters, a small mountainous mass with a surface area of no more than 25 square kilometres. Mountains form the heart of this land, where twisting roads wind their way up to a series of villages. The villages' few and charmingly-kept houses are surrounded by stunted vegetation that strains to grow in the poor volcanic soil, bereft of both lakes and rivers. The island's terrain is similar to that of Saint Martin's, with great salt-water ponds dotting its terrain. It also boasts the magnificent beaches and idyllic panoramas that are part of the precious heritage of this French land.

The islands of Saint Martin and Saint Barts are swept by trade winds that blow from east to west over the Atlantic Ocean, carrying humid air with them. When this wind comes in contact with the islands' sheer mountainsides, the moisture-laden air condenses and turns into rain. Their eastern coasts, known as *côtes-au-vent* or windward coasts, are thus subjected to sudden downpours, allowing verdant vegetation to flourish

Typhoons, Cyclones and Hurricanes

Whether dealing with typhoons in Asia, cyclones in the southwestern part of the Indian Ocean or hurricanes in the Caribbean Sea, it is always a question of the same phenomenon: that is, a tropical (atmospheric) disturbance. Such disturbances are formed by the presence of large expanses of water at temperatures exceeding 26°C that span depths of several dozen metres. Hurricanes travel from east to west, accompanied by violent winds with velocities of over 120 kph; they sometimes hit islands and cause considerable damage. This is what occurred in 1995, when Hurricane Luis, one of the most powerful recorded hurricanes in the 20th century, swept the coasts of Saint Martin and Saint Barts, destroying vegetation and devastating towns and hamlets alike. The inhabitants recovered quickly from this unbelievably intense natural disaster, and construction work was soon undertaken. Today, the traces of hurricane Luis have been more or less eradicated, and only the Dutch side of Saint Martin (Sint Maarten) still bears a few scars.

here. Their western coasts, which face the Caribbean Sea, are sheltered from these winds by the very same mountains and are called *côtes-sous-le-vent*, or leeward coasts. Rarely subjected to sudden downpours, the vegetation growing on the west coasts is stunted and essentially composed of scrubs and cacti.

FLORA

Though the windward coasts are covered in lush vegetation, most areas of these two Caribbean islands have only stunted flora because of the arid climate. Shrubs and cacti do their utmost to cling to the poor soil of steep hillsides and, in certain places, plants seem to grow out of the very rock.

Nevertheless, this scenery is teeming with multi-coloured flora. The incredibly vibrant flowers grow all year round, brightening the landscape with reds, pinks and brilliant yellows. Hibiscus,

Palm Trees

Tall, stately palm trees dot the landscape of the Lesser Antilles. There are 2,779 varieties of this tree, which belongs to the monocotyledonous family. It grows in humid forests and deserts alike, and can be found both in coastal regions and in the mountains. Except for palm creepers, all the species are similar. Their stalks, which are almost the same in diameter at the base as at the top, are not trunks, but rather stipe that end in a fountain of leaves. The new leaves grow out of the middle of this "bouquet", while the old leaves fall off, revealing the stalk.

Some species of palms are used for multiple purposes, for example them the royal palm, the red latan and the coconut palm, whose stems are used in construction, and whose fruits (coconuts) are a popular food. Palm fronds are also used for roofing and to make hats.

pink laurels, ballisiers, orchids and alpinias adorn gardens and parks. Trees and shrubs, bougainvilleas and poinciana, among others, complete this luxuriant and utterly enchanting tableau with their flower-laden branches.

Unique flora grows in some areas along the coast, not to mention the marine vegetation that divers encounter in the deep.

Coastal Landscapes

Magnificent stretches of white sandy beaches border much of the coast of Saint Barts and Saint Martin; some, such as the glorious Orient Bay, are over a kilometre long. A particular type of vegetation flourishes along the edge of the beaches. It is essentially composed of sea-grape trees, easily recognizable by their clusters of large green fruit similar to grapes, as well as creeping lianas and palm trees. Another tree occasionally found near beaches is the dangerous manchineel, distinguished by its small, green round leaves bisected by a yellow vein. These trees are generally marked by a red X or a warning sign, because they produce poisonous sap that can cause serious burns.

The Mangrove Swamp

This strange forest, growing in salt water and mud, consists mainly of mangroves (the most common being the red mangrove, recognizable by its aerial roots). Shrubs and plants also thrive in this swampland and, farther inland, the river mangrove develops in less briny waters. A vast quantity of organisms such as birds, crustaceans and, above all, a multitude of insects of all kinds, live in the heart of this impenetrable forest. This complex and fragile ecosystem plays an essential role for the islands' fauna as it provides both nourishment and shelter. In Saint Martin, to the south of Orient Bay, the Baie de l'Embouchure offers a distant view of a mangrove swamp that was damaged by Hurricane Luis in 1995, and is slowly growing back.

FAUNA

As in other parts of the Lesser Antilles that have never been connected to the American continent, wildlife is not very diverse on these volcanic islands sprung from the sea. In fact, the mammals that have proliferated here were all introduced by humans. Among these is the mongoose, introduced by European colonists in an effort to eliminate rats and venomous snakes (water moccasins) that destroyed crops. The mongoose also attacked various indigenous species, particularly ground-nesting birds that until then had no predators, and exterminated many of them.

Animal life is nevertheless abundant on the islands, and reptiles notably are especially plentiful. Lizards, among others the anole, ground anole, and Mabuya, are among the species that have evolved on these sun-drenched soils. These insectivores and omnivores can attain a maximum length of 30 centimetres. **Iguanas**, which feed on plants and insects, are much larger and can grow to lengths of up to one metre. Although they can look intimidating, they are perfectly harmless.

Birds

Winged wildlife abounds on the islands, making a bird-watcher out of just about anyone who looks around. To help you identify these animals, we have included a description of the most common species below. With a bit of patience and a good pair of binoculars, you are sure to spot a few.

The **brown pelican** has greyish-brown plumage and is distinguished by its long neck and long grey beak with a large pouch. It is usually seen alone or in small groups, flying in single file. These birds, which can grow to up to 140 centimetres, are commonly found near beaches.

The wingspan of the jet-black **magnificent frigate bird** can reach up to 2.5 metres. The colour of the throat is the distinguishing mark between the sexes; the male's is red, the female's white. These birds can often be spotted gliding effortlessly over the waves in search of food.

Brown Pelican   *Magnificent Frigate Bird*

The **kingfisher** is found in eastern North America and the Lesser Antilles. It is set apart by its blue plumage and white breast, but more specifically by its large head topped with a crested tuft. It can often be seen practically hovering in one spot before plunging into the waves in search of food.

Cattle Egret   *Green heron*

Herons are often found wading near mangrove swamps and fresh-water ponds. Among the different types is the **great heron**, which can grow to up to 132 centimetres in height. It is identifiable by the large black feather extending from its white head down its neck. Its body is covered with grey and white plumage. You'll certainly spot the **cattle egret**, another bird in the same family commonly seen in the fields amongst the cattle. This bird is about 60 centimetres tall, with white plumage and an orange tuft of feathers on its head. It arrived in the Caribbean during the 1950s; before that it was spotted only in Africa. It has adapted well and is found in large numbers throughout the Antilles. Finally, you'll probably hear the distinctive call of the little **green heron**. This bird grows to a height of 45 centimetres and has greenish-grey feathers on its back and wings.

Visitors can catch a glimpse of the **black-necked stilt**, a wader measuring about 35 centimetres in height, in the marshes and in the vicinity of the mangrove swamp. It is distinguished by its black back, wings, beak the upper part of its head (including its eyes) which contrasts with its white underbelly and lower part of its head. Its legs are very thin and pink.

The **bananaquit**, also known as the yellow-breasted sunbird, is a small bird, about 10 centimetres tall, found throughout the Lesser Antilles. It is easily identifiable by its dark grey or black upper parts and its yellow throat and breast. It feeds on nectar and juice from various fruits including bananas and papaya. This greedy little bird often sets down on a patio table for a bit of sugar.

Black-necked stilt   *Bananaquit*

The minuscule **hummingbird**, with its colourful plumage, feeds on insects and nectar and can be seen hovering about near flowering bushes and trees. Two types of hummingbird live on these islands. The **green-throated carib** can grow to up to 12 centimetres and has black plumage with green iridescent feathers on its head and throat. The **antillean crested humming-bird**, the smallest hummingbird weighing no more than two grams, has a blue and green crest.

There are several types of turtledove on the islands, each about the size of a pigeon. The most common is the **zenaida dove**, with a brown back and a pinkish-beige breast, neck and head. It also has a blue spot on either side of its head. The **common turtledove** has greyish-brown plumage, with a black and white speckled neck.

The Ocean Floor

The shallow, perpetually warm waters (20°C) around the islands provide a perfect environment for the growth of **coral**. Formed by a colony of minuscule organisms called coelenterate polyps growing on a polypary (calcareous skeleton), coral takes many different forms. These coral colonies have developed along the leeward coasts, protected from violent winds. The abundance of plankton around these formations attracts a wide variety of marine wildlife. Fish of all sizes also gravitate around the coral, including **tuna**, **kingfish**, more colourful fish like **parrot-fish**, **boxfish**, **mullet**, **angel-fish** and on rare occasions **sharks**. The coral is also home to numerous other animals, like **sponges** and **sea urchins**.

HISTORY

Natives had settled in the Antilles long before Columbus ever discovered the New World. Much like other indigenous peoples, their ancestors came from northern Asia, crossing the Bering Strait toward the end of the ice age before inhabiting practically all of the Americas in successive migratory waves. Because of the Caribbean's geographical isolation, it was only later that these people ventured there.

Evidence suggests that the Ciboney, the first Arawak-speaking tribe to undertake the long voyage to the Caribbean Islands, arrived in Saint Martin over 3,500 years ago. A thousand years later, a second wave of Arawak-speaking Andean natives, the Huécoïdes, apparently came and settled here. The next group to reach the island was the Saladoïdes, also Arawak-speaking. This last group then migrated to the Dominican Republic, where it very likely encountered descendants of the Ciboneys. These two groups mingled (henceforth named "modified Saladoïdes") and returned to settle in Saint Martin between AD 800 and 1200. A fishing people, they built their villages by the sea, from which they drew the greater part of their food. Relics, notably shards of clay pottery, found on the island of Saint Martin bear witness to these ancient origins and migratory movements as well as to its inhabitants' dexterity and skill.

For centuries, these Arawak-speaking tribes were the sole rulers of the islands, until another group, the Caribs (the fourth migratory wave from South America, from the region between the Orinoco and Amazon rivers), set their sights on this region. A fierce war was then waged against the Arawaks, who, being ill-equipped to defend themselves, were unable to hold out against their foes and abandoned certain territories. Indeed, the Caribs came to control the whole of the Lesser Antilles. They came to Saint Barts to fish for shellfish. It seems, however, that none went to Saint Martin. Archaeological digs of Caribbean sites of the Lesser Antilles attest to the fact that this group, known for its mastery in the making of weapons, particularly axes, did not inherit the artistic skills of its predecessors.

Discovery of the Antilles

On the morning of August 3, 1492, Christopher Columbus, financed by the Catholic kings of Spain and Aragon, headed a flotilla of three caravels, the *Santa Maria*, the *Pinta* and the *Niña*, and undertook a voyage west in search of a new route to Asia. This two-month voyage across the Atlantic Ocean led him to the Caribbean archipelago, more specifically to one of the islands of the Bahamas known to natives as "Guanahani". Thus marking the official "discovery" of the Americas on October 12th, 1492, Columbus and his men believed themselves to be just off the coast of Southeast Asia.

For a few weeks, Columbus and his crew explored Guanahani and the surrounding islands, establishing the first links with the natives. He then continued on his way toward Cuba, skirting its coast. The Genoese sailor then proceeded toward the coast of another island, known to natives as "Tohio", which he named "Isla Espagnola" (or Hispaniola). Following the coast and exploring part of this island, which he found magnificent, he soon envisaged the possibility of establishing a Spanish colony there. The shipwreck of the *Santa Maria* provided a perfect excuse to erect a fort here. A few weeks later, Columbus, fired with enthusiasm, returned to Spain, leaving 39 soldiers behind.

About ten months elapsed before Columbus undertook a second voyage to the Americas. Upon his return to Hispaniola, he found no trace of the fort or the soldiers; they had been slaughtered by the natives. Might the soldiers have abused the natives' hospitality? Whatever the case, punitive expeditions against the natives were undertaken as a result. Columbus, having returned with the necessary materials and men to found a Spanish city, did not allow himself to be discouraged by the incident, and proceeded to found the island's first city.

The natives of this island, the Arawaks, told Columbus of tribes on the other islands to the south, prompting him to continue exploring in that direction, thus discovering the chain of islands now known as the Lesser Antilles. The Genoese sailor remained undaunted by the lack of potable water and the Caribs, the islands' inhabitants who were prepared to fiercely defend their territory. He landed on several islands, including Dominica, and then continued on to Guadeloupe where he stayed for a time to replenish his stock of fresh water. He then took to the sea once again, heading north, where he came across Saint Barts, which he named after his bother Bartolomé. On November 11, 1493, Saint Martin's Day, he happened upon yet another small island, which he named in honour of the saint.

No doubt due to the lack of men needed to populate all these new lands and because of the Caribs who inhabited them, the Spanish decided not to colonize the Lesser Antilles but, rather, to concentrate their efforts on the Greater Antilles. Many years passed before a colony was established in the Lesser Antilles. In the meantime, the islands served mainly as stopping points for the privateers and sailors navigating these waters.

The Birth of the West Indian Colonies

Only the Spanish and Portuguese succeeded in colonizing the New World in the 15th century. Their boats arrived in Europe full of treasures taken from native American peoples and quickly became targeted by smugglers and pirates who crisscrossed the seas, looting them for the spoils. It was these treasures plundered from the Spanish that showed the rest of Europe the riches to be reaped by claiming these lands to the west.

Around 1623, the French privateer D'Esnambuc sailed for the Lesser Antilles. After having attacked the Spanish at sea, he sought refuge on Saint-Christophe to repair his vessel. The English navigator Warner was already on the island, but the two managed to divide the territory among themselves. Upon his return to France, d'Esnambuc had these boundaries ratified, and founded the *Compagnie Saint-Christophe* under the patronage of Richelieu, who had a high-ranking administrative position and was in charge of the exploitation of new territories, and also held trading rights.

During the following years, France pursued the colonization of the Lesser Antilles much more aggressively. The *Compagnie des Îles d'Amérique* replaced the *Compagnie Saint-Christophe* in 1635, with a mandate to conquer the territories situated between 10° and 30° latitude north.

France, however, was not the only European power with an eye on the Antilles; the Dutch were also attempting to colonize the islands. In 1621, the first Dutch company was created. Known as the West Indies Company (Colbert created another company with the same name in later years), it undertook the conquest of several islands in the Lesser Antilles, including Saint Martin, Aruba, Bonaire and Curaçao. In 1638, the Dutch built a fort on Saint Martin, having found significant salt deposits on the island.

Saint Martin was quickly reconquered by the Spanish, who wanted to maintain control of the island, since it was a stopping point for many ships. In 1638, 9,000 Spanish soldiers were sent to supervise the territory. This manoeuvre quickly proved less strategic than the Spanish had thought; realizing the futility of their actions, they abandoned the island less than ten years later, leaving the field wide open for other colonists.

Colonization

Little by little, the conquest of the Lesser Antilles was undertaken by the French. Two men, Liénart de l'Olive and du Plessis, convinced the *Compagnie des Îles d'Amérique* of the necessity of colonizing Guadeloupe. Accompanied by 500 men and a few representatives of the church (including Père Duterte), they arrived on June 28, 1635. Acclimatization proved difficult, however, and the men suffered from a lack of supplies, epidemics and famine. Establishing this new colony also entailed waging a brutal war against the Caribs, which further hampered colonists' efforts.

The first attempt at colonizing Guadeloupe changed nothing with respect to the administration of the territories, and the seat of the French colonies remained in Saint-Christophe (present-day Saint Kitts). In 1638, following the death of Liénart de l'Olive and du Plessis, Poincy de Lonvilliers, then governor, devised a plan to transfer the capital (Saint-Christophe) to Guadeloupe. This move would have favoured the latter's development had it not been thwarted by conflicts between the governor's personal ambitions, the interests of the *Compagnie* executives back in France and those of the other representatives in the islands.

The Partition of Saint Martin

Apparently, the partition of Saint Martin was brought about very simply: two men were dispatched from opposite sides of the island and the point at which they met determined the dividing line. France thus acquired three fifths of the island, while the Netherlands procured a smaller portion, but one that had greater natural resources.

This period of instability did nothing to reassure the colonists of Saint-Christophe, and some, considering the situation precarious, decided to try their luck elsewhere. Thus, four French colonists left Saint-Christophe in 1648, disembarking on Saint Martin with the aim of settling there. They were not alone in coveting the island abandoned by Spanish troops, however, for the Dutch government, having the same designs, had sent Martin Thomas to take possession of the territory. Rather than engaging in ruthless warfare, these new arrivals opted for an equitable partition of the island on the 24th of March, 1648. The accord to this effect was signed on March 24, 1648, on a mountain henceforth known as *"Mont des Accords"*.

That same year, convinced of the importance of colonizing each of the islets in the Lesser Antilles, Poincy de Lonvilliers sent Sieur Jacques de Gente along with about 50 colonists to populate Saint Barts. Devoid of lakes and rivers and possessing poor soil, the island had everything to discourage these new arrivals who, left to themselves, had to persevere in order to survive.

Agreements aimed at ending the war between the French and the Caribs were reached at this time (1641), and the colony experienced a period of peace. The respite was welcomed by the colonists, who needed time to get settled, and by the *Compagnie des Îles d'Amérique*, which found the colonies expensive. Famine, war against the Caribs, bad weather and countless other problems eventually forced the company to sell its possessions. It sold Saint-Christophe in 1647, and then gave up its other islands. Along with Saint Barts, Saint-Martin became a possession of the Order of Malta in 1651.

The Order of Malta

Originally called the "Knights of the Hospital of Saint John of Jerusalem", the Order of Malta was founded during the Crusades to protect and care for pilgrims on their way to Palestine (AD 1113). Despite their active role in the Crusades, the knights had to withdraw when the Holy Land was lost. The Order thus relocated to Cyprus. It wasn't until 1530, when Charles V gave up the island of Malta, that these knights took the name "the knights of Malta". By the time Saint Martin was purchased, the Order was rich and powerful.

This change of administration resulted in little change for the colonists; they still had to endure difficult living conditions and the hostility of the native population, which was fiercely set on preserving its land. Cohabitation between these two communities was difficult, and the slightest indiscretion became a source of violent conflict. Indeed, the inhabitants of Saint Barts paid the price in 1656, when the Caribs, bent on revenge against the colonists, undertook various reprisals against the French colonies and, upon reaching the shores of Saint Barts, slaughtered all its inhabitants. Its colony annihilated, the island was abandoned for close to four years. Despite this blow, the will to colonize it remained steadfast and the island was repopulated in 1659 when a second group of Bretons, Normans and Poitevins came to settle there.

These Caribbean colonies developed gradually despite early obstacles and a precarious economic situation. In order to encourage their growth, Colbert, who began attending to the French kingdom's affairs in 1661, decided to create a powerful company backed by the king, which would manage all the colonies. The *Compagnie des Indes Occidentales* was thus founded on May 13, 1664. On July 10th of the same year, Guadeloupe, Martinique and Saint-Christophe were acquired by the company; the following year, Saint-Martin (the French side) and Saint Barts were purchased as well. Colbert's intentions were not fully realized, however, because, although the company had a monopoly on trade between these islands and France's colonies in the Americas, it was deemed too unprofitable and was forced to cease operations. In 1674, the company's possessions were transferred to the French Crown.

Through these difficult first 50 years of colonization, the French and the Dutch succeeded in establishing themselves in the Antilles. This, however, had harsh consequences for the Carib and Arawak populations, which were ruthlessly attacked by the colonists seeking to appropriate their lands. Not numerous enough to resist these foreign offensives, the Caribs were decimated and the Arawaks exterminated. In 1660, the last Caribs were expelled from all French possessions and relocated in Dominica and Saint Vincent. Their descendants still live in Dominica today.

The Emergence of a Distinct Caribbean Economy

While the governors tried to get richer, newly arrived colonists in the Antilles had to settle in and develop greater self-sufficiency, since it was always difficult to secure supplies from France. Crops like yams, peas, indigo, tobacco and cotton provided food and modest revenue from trade with France.

The introduction of sugar cane to the Antilles (around 1650 in Saint Martin) shook up the island's economy, as sugar was becoming more and more prized on the European market, making for handsome returns for the colonists. A problem quickly presented itself to farmers though: harvesting sugar cane requires a large workforce. There were not enough inhabitants on the island at the time, so efforts were made to increase the population. At first, the leaders of the colonies tried to attract French farmers by setting up a recruitment program. The program was very demanding for future colonists, who had to sign up for 36 months. During this time they could not enter into any contracts and essentially signed over their freedom and their labour to their master. In exchange they received a piece of land or sum of money at the end of the contract. The horrible living conditions of the recruits (poor treatment, insufficient food, sickness) in most cases led to death or abandonment before the end of the term. It is therefore no surprise that, as of 1668, the recruitment of French workers was practically non-existent. Another solution would have to be found to the workforce problem.

Slavery was quickly presented as the only inexpensive solution, and colonists set their sights on the coast of western Africa, from where countless Africans were taken by force and shipped off to the Antilles. These men and women, sent by sea in the most horrible and inhumane conditions (many of them died en route), arrived in Saint Martin. Sold to landowning colonists, they soon formed a large workforce.

The introduction of slavery thus enabled the people of Saint Martin to undertake the cultivation of sugar cane and, though the arid land received little rain and the crops' yield proved somewhat meagre, the inhabitants prospered. This growth, however, was restricted by limits imposed by the mother countries, who did not want the islands' commodities to compete with the products of French and Dutch farmers.

With the passing years, the population of black slaves grew considerably, and soon made up the majority of the sugar islands' (Saint Martin, Guadeloupe, Martinique) inhabitants, resulting in major social tensions. In an effort to counter the "dangers" of a black-slave majority, harsh policies were adopted to control the slaves. This, of course, did little to appease the people's anger, as the number of uprisings in this period show.

Saint Barts: An Exceptional History

Much like Guadeloupe and Martinique, Saint Martin succeeded in developing an economy based on the sale of sugar cane. Conversely, Saint Barts, whose soil proved too poor to support this type of cultivation, was deprived of the prosperity enjoyed by its sister islands; its inhabitants had to content themselves with farming, which just barely provided for their needs. Their lives were made all the more difficult by the frequent and devastating foreign incursions besetting their land, which was practically indefensible and consequently devoid of garrisons. Enemy troops were not alone in coveting this islet: early on, privateers and pirates saw it as an ideal refuge. Though somewhat questionable, these new arrivals were nevertheless able to trade with the inhabitants, which led to their cohabitation: the privateers benefited from Anse du Carénage (as Gustavia was once known; *carénage* is the French word for careenage, a place to careen, or tip, a boat in order to clean its hull), while the residents of Saint Barts withdrew into the island's interior.

This strange proximity was not, however, without conse-quences for the small colony, for several denizens of Saint Barts, exasperated by foreign attacks, chose to become pirates as well and pillaged foreign vessels skirting the coast. This new activity around the coast of Saint Barts enabled the small colony to grow, and a village soon grew around Carénage.

This modest boom only lasted about twenty years, however, for the English, exasperated by the frequent assaults, attacked the island in 1744, capturing the privateers and replacing them with their own, who pillaged and slaughtered the remaining inhabitants. A little later, the British governor, condemning the excesses of his troops, allowed the survivors who had managed to find refuge on Saint-Christophe to return to their island.

Nevertheless, the citizens of Saint Barts had little respite from their troubles, for, in the course of the 18th century, devastat-ing foreign incursions were numerous and, much like France's other possessions (including Saint-Martin), their island was brought under British control on more than one occasion. At the end of the Seven Years War (Treaty of Paris, 1763), France lost out to the British and was forced to surrender some of its colonies. In order to keep its profitable sugar-producing colonies of Martinique, Guadeloupe and Saint-Martin (Saint Barts was also restored to France due to an oversight in the treaty), France abandoned its possessions in North America.

Saint Martin and the Slow March to Emancipation

The end of the 18th century was a particularly turbulent time for Saint Martin, Guadeloupe and Martinique, as much due to instability caused by foreign incursions as to racial tensions that were reaching their peak. Such was the explosive context in the Antilles when the French Revolution occurred in 1789, leading to the abolition of the monarchy. This considerable upheaval that struck France had its consequences in the islands, as well as certain large property owners saw an opportunity to end the trade restrictions imposed by the French government, thus giving the colony greater autonomy. At the same time, anti-slavery movements came up against owners who favoured a hard line on slaves. Finally, the small property-owners anticipated playing a more important political role, thereby getting out from under the yoke of the large property-owners and the aristocrats. All of this dissent exploded in the wake of the events of 1789.

In February, 1794, English troops arrived in Martinique, Guadeloupe and Saint-Martin and took advantage of this internal disorder to overthrow the existing administration. Victor Hugues was sent to Guadeloupe to counter the English invasion. Along with 14 frigates and 18 warships full of men, Hugues was backed by all the black slaves, to whom he had promised freedom. Hugues arrived in Guadeloupe in June, and by December had succeeded in pushing back the English. Saint-Martin was liberated in 1796, and Hugues took this opportunity to annex the Dutch part of the island, which France would keep until 1801.

During this period, the slaves were set free. Their liberty did not last long, however, as bit by bit the governors that followed Hugues revoked the rights accorded the blacks. Under Napoleon's government, slavery was actually reinstated.

The island of Saint Martin fell once more to English conquerors, who occupied the island in 1808 and ruled it until 1815. The signing of the Treaty of Vienna put an end to Caribbean rivalries between these two European powers. Peace was thus restored to the small colony, which progressively changed as anti-slavery movements mobilized; slavery was abolished in British colonies as of 1833. The abolition of slavery in the French colonies was not instituted until 1848, however, when an official decree was initiated by Victor Schœlcher. Slaves inhabiting the Dutch part of Saint Martin were not freed until 1863.

The abolition of slavery had major consequences for residents of Saint Martin. Living conditions for recently-freed blacks remained precarious, and the whole economy had to be restructured in order to provide wages for this previously unpaid workforce. This restructuring raised the production costs of sugar, thus causing a major crisis in the industry. In order to remedy this delicate economic situation, large sugar companies were formed through small mergers, thereby offering jobs to the local workforce. As a result, many of the smaller farmers were forced into bankruptcy. Sugar cane production nevertheless remained difficult in Saint Martin due to lack of rain and water, and local inhabitants gradually gave up. The island's salt reserves and status as a free port, acquired in 1850, led sailors to use its port installations and brought in the bulk of its meagre revenue.

Saint Barts and Nearly a Century of Swedish Colonization

The few hundred years leading to the liberation of slaves in Caribbean colonies were quite different in Saint Barts, where there were virtually no slaves. This period was particularly distinct due to the fact that the island was sold to Sweden in 1785 by King Louis XVI, who deemed it more profitable to have the right to trade with Sweden (he acquired a warehouse in Gothenburg in exchange) than to keep this arid land.

This exchange proved beneficial for the residents of Saint Barts, at least as far as their economy was concerned, for a number of favourable policies were adopted on their behalf. Carénage, the island's port, was renamed "Gustavia" (in honour of the Swedish king, Gustave III) in 1785 by governor Salomon Mauritz von Rayalin, and became a free port. A few years later, when the inhabitants' poverty came to his attention, Gustave III granted them tax exemptions. The period between 1795 and 1820 was particularly prosperous thanks to greatly increased activity at the port. Despite this newfound affluence, however, the inhabitants of Saint Barts of French origin had trouble accepting this new authority. They kept to themselves, rarely mingled with Swedes and refused to submit to the Swedish governors.

This wealth, however, was only to last about twenty years, for, after 1820, Saint Barts' port was abandoned in favour of other islands, precipitating yet another economic decline. Moreover, the island was rocked by a series of natural disasters, making it a far less attractive possession. Furthermore, the inhabitants were already so poor that, in the days following the abolition of slavery, no one could afford to pay their workers, and the few

Important Dates in the History of Saint Barts and Saint Martin

1493: Christopher Columbus discovers the Lesser Antilles, including Guadeloupe, Marie-Galante, La Désirade, Les Saintes, Saint Barts and Saint Martin. At the time, the islands are inhabited by Caribs.

1635: The *Compagnie de Saint-Christophe* gets French colonization underway in the Caribbean.

1638: Spanish troops entrench themselves on Saint Martin.

1648: Saint Martin is colonized by the French and the Dutch, who share the territory. A first group of colonists settles on Saint Barts, but is massacred by the Caribs.

1651: Saint Martin becomes a possession of the Order of Malta.

1659: A second contingent of Bretons, Normans and Poitevins establish themselves on Saint Barts.

1660: The Carib people are decimated or deported from the French territories to Dominica.

1664: The Order of Malta sells its Caribbean possessions to the *Compagnie des Indes Occidentales*, founded by Colbert.

1674: Following the bankruptcy of the *Compagnie des Indes Occidentales*, the Caribbean possessions become attached to the French Crown.

Late 17th century: African people are brought to the islands as slaves.

1785: Saint Barts is sold to the Swedish for the French right to trade in Swedish territory.

1789: Revolution rocks France with important consequences for the administration of the colonies. The slaves are freed.

1802: Napoleon's troops land on Saint Martin and re-establish slavery.

1848: Slavery is definitively abolished in the French Antilles.

1877: Sweden cedes Saint Barts back to France.

1946: Guadeloupe and Martinique become overseas French departments. Saint Barts and Saint-Martin are administratively tied to Guadeloupe.

1995: Hurricane Luis hits Saint Martin and Saint Barts.

freed slaves, having no other resources, had no choice but to seek exile.

During the 19th century, the situation on the island was such that the Swedish government saw no advantage in keeping it and sought to relinquish it. Saint Barts was thus ceded back to France on August 10, 1877, in exchange for a sum of 400,000 francs and the obligation to leave its residents exempt from taxes, a situation that has remained unchanged to this day. This treaty was ratified by the great majority of the population, which became French once again. The island was administratively tied to Guadeloupe, which also comprised the French portion of Saint Martin.

The End of the 19th and the 20th Centuries

In 1877, Saint Barts was grafted to the other French Antillean colonies, which had just survived years that were at best difficult and some of which had seen their economies completely collapse. In Saint Martin the gains drawn from the sugar trade had disappeared and the island's sole source of revenue was its port facilities. The people of Saint Barts survived on the modest returns from agriculture and fishing.

The 20th century brought its own lot of hardships. The outbreak of the Great War in 1914 had major repercussions for Saint-Martin and Saint Barts, which sent their own contingents of soldiers to support France's efforts. The Netherlands remained neutral throughout this conflict.

Between the two wars, the two tax-exempt islands' economies prospered. Commerce and trade in general, but especially of tobacco and liquor, were favoured. In fact, the islands were a central part of the illegal liquor trade during the years of prohibition in the United States.

Before long, another catastrophe rocked Europe: the Second World War, which began on September 3, 1939. Less than a year later the Netherlands (May 10, 1940) and France (June 16, 1940) fell to the Germans, but the administrative consequences were negligible for the islands. Both countries were liberated in 1945.

On March 19, 1946, an important law concerning Guadeloupe, its dependencies and Martinique was adopted, when these colonies were established as overseas French departments or *départements français d'outre-mer*. The French side of Saint Martin became part of the department of Guadeloupe. Both islands experienced significant economic development thanks to the growth of the tourism industry, which flourished from the beginning of the 1980s.

ECONOMY

The arid soil of Saint Martin, and particularly that of Saint Barts, prevented the two little islands from ever experiencing the boom brought on by the sugar industry. In Saint Martin, the cultivation of sugar cane was possible, but never productive enough, and had to be abandoned in the 19th century when a crisis in the sugar industry compromised any prospect of profit. The inhabitants of Saint Barts, meanwhile, were obliged to fall back on the cultivation of a handful of crops like cotton and then pineapple in the 19th century, which just barely allowed the colonists to remain self-sufficient. Over the years, other industries such as fishing, salt mining (from rich deposits on the Dutch side of Saint Martin) and port infrastructures enabled the inhabitants to improve their living conditions, though they never ensured their prosperity.

Nevertheless, these little islands in the north of the archipelago, administratively tied to Guadeloupe that itself still had a ways to go in structuring its own economy, were too often neglected and could never count on its help. The Dutch part of the island, Sint Maarten, experienced similar economic difficulties due because of its distance from other Dutch properties. On several occasions, the Dutch inhabitants preferred seeking exile further south, on the islands of Aruba and Curaçao, which had more to offer.

The 20th century brought more prosperous times. First, the construction of the Princess Juliana airport (Sint Maarten) allowed the island to develop better relations with its neighbours, most importantly the United States. Next, the Dutch part of Saint Martin became a tax haven and profited from considerable foreign investment, which led to the expansion of its tourist industry. Sint Maarten's tourist industry was so huge that the Dutch territory welcomed the most tourists (500,000 in 1995) of all the Lesser Antilles. In its shadow, Saint-Martin, which thrived because of its status as a free port, also saw its tourist industry develop into one of the mainstays of its economy. Saint Barts, whose residents have been free from taxation since 1785 (a measure implemented in response to their extreme poverty), also presents undeniable advantages attractive to investors. At the beginning of the 1980s it also saw important growth in the tourism industry. Given the small size of its territory, Saint Barts has always successfully catered to wealthy visitors. Both islands live with and by the comings and goings of tourists, attracted by their sunny beaches and natural setting. Though some have profited from the tourism boom, there is still a large disparity on Saint Martin between the rich French, Dutch and foreign minority and the working-class majority, who live in very modest conditions.

POLITICAL INSTITUTIONS

Saint Martin and Saint Barts

Since the law of March 19, 1946 came into effect, Guadeloupe has been a *département français d'outre-mer* or DOM, and Saint-Martin and Saint Barts, have been designated *cantons*. In

1963, Saint-Martin was elevated to a *sous-préfecture* (the *sous-préfecture* of the northern islands is made up of Saint-Martin, Tintamarre and Saint-Barthélemy). In accordance with the constitution, they have two political assemblies: the *Conseil Régional*, based on a system of proportional representation, and the *Conseil Général*, elected by a two-round majority vote. The *Conseil Régional* handles economic and regional development and workforce training, while the *Conseil Général* looks after social concerns. These two assemblies have the power to legislate within their respective domains and determine appropriate budgets as well. Besides the *Conseil Régional* and the *Conseil Général*, the department has a *Comité Économique et Social* and a *Comité de la Culture et de l'Evironnement*. Four deputies represent the department in the French *Assemblée Nationale*, and two senators in the *Sénat*.

Citizens of the French section of Saint Martin, as well as those of Saint Barts, enjoy the same social programs as citizens of France, including old age pensions, family allowances, unemployment insurance and health insurance. However, these programs are not always administered in the same way here as they are in continental Europe.

During the last few decades, politics in the French overseas department of Guadeloupe, of which Saint-Martin and Saint Barts are a part, have been particularly marked by demands for autonomy from the mother country. However, since the social structure of Saint-Martin and Saint Barts is very different from that of Guadeloupe itself, these two islands' populations have never been in favour of separation, at the very most wanting greater economic independence.

Sint Maarten

Sint Maarten is part of the kingdom of the Netherlands, and its inhabitants are subjected to a very different political system than that of the French side of the island, since the Netherlands granted it full autonomy in internal affairs. The kingdom encompasses three countries: the Netherlands proper, and the overseas departments of Aruba and the Netherlands Antilles, the latter of which include Bonaire, Curaçao, Saba, Sint Eustatius and Sint Maarten. Though they remain dependencies, each of these countries has its own parliament elected by popular vote, as well as a Cabinet and a prime minister. The government has the power to legislate and is responsible for local affairs, including social and medical services, education, economic development, road maintenance, tourism promotion and sports. It also oversees water and electricity distribution as well as port and airport installations, which are run by state-sponsored companies. Foreign affairs, defence and judicial affairs remain the responsibility of the kingdom of the Netherlands.

Thus, unlike the French part of the island, Sint Maarten creates its own policy on issues related to its development, most notably its social programs. This greater level of autonomy means that Sint Maarten's social programs are not necessarily the same as those of the Netherlands.

PORTRAIT

POPULATION

The flourishing economy, the sun and Saint Martin's status as a free port have attracted many immigrants to the island. In fact, the population is growing by leaps and bounds, increasing from 10,000 (in either part of the island) at the beginning of the 1980s to nearly 30,000 in the French part and more than 39,000 in Dutch part in about 15 years. To these official numbers must be added between 5,000 and 30,000 illegal residents (the coasts are hard to supervise) living on the island. Such foreigners have swelled the ranks of the rich immigrants who make up only a tiny portion of newcomers to the island. People have come from many different countries; it is said that 70 nationalities are represented on the island. In fact, there are so many immigrants, that Creoles no longer form a majority on this little island.

It is a completely different story in Saint Barts, where 95% of its approximately 5,000 inhabitants are white, many of them of Norman, Breton or Poitevin descent. Long isolated, this tiny society has a reputation for being very closed and not very welcoming to new arrivals. Indeed, it does everything possible to counter the arrival of illegal foreign workers on its territory.

CULTURE

Saint Martin

The increasing influence of the United States, which has characterized the second half of the 20th century, has led to the Americanization of local culture here as in other places. Saint Martin has had more contact with this giant than its sister island, Guadeloupe. Moreover, the mother tongue of a good many locals is no longer French or Dutch, but English. The massive influx of immigrants and tourists has also played a great part in shaping a very different society on this Caribbean island. It is therefore no longer a predominantly Creole culture as was once the case, but rather a multiethnic one.

Saint Barts

Because of its history and demographics, Saint Barts stands apart from the other French Caribbean islands. The cultural mingling so characteristic of the Antilles never occurred here; its inhabitants are primarily of French extraction. Long isolated from the metropolis just as they were from other Caribbean islands, and having inherited barren soil, the inhabitants of Saint Barts have persevered throughout the centuries and resisted foreign occupations while preserving the essentials of their French heritage. Their language is peppered with certain archaisms and terms borrowed from the vocabulary of sailors, so much a legacy of their Breton, Norman, Vendée or Poitevin ancestors. Surprisingly, the population fought to stay on the island for decades, despite the difficulties of living here. Traditionally, its men have sought work on other islands, but have always retained Saint Barts as their home and kept their families here. Is it any wonder, then, that this small community has the reputation for being closed and exclusive to this day?

The Architecture of the Creole Cottage

Though the wood cottages scattered throughout Saint Martin and Saint Barts may appear quite fragile, they were designed to withstand the capricious climate of the Caribbean islands. Comprising two to three rooms and rarely measuring over 21 square metres, the wooden Creole cottage is the most common dwelling here. These houses were built on sites carefully chosen to ensure their solidity. Before assembling the framework, a stone foundation was laid out to protect the wood from dampness. Four pillars were then erected (at each corner of the house), after which the frame was raised. Overlaid with wooden planks, some had the advantage of being sided with wooden shingles (called *essentes* here) making them more watertight. The roof was made of dried grasses or palm fronds, or shingles, according to the occupant's means. All the wooden pieces could be easily dismantled, making them easier to move, for, though most people owned their cottages, they often did not own the land on which they were built.

Today, wooden cottages, whose architecture is largely inspired by the wooden Creole cottage, are still built but are painted with lovely colours and often embellished with lacy wood trim, balconies and shutters. Indeed, all these ornaments make these living quarters quite pleasant.

In Saint Barts, a type of dwelling particular to its windward side, called the *cabrette*, is designed to withstand the occasionally violent winds blowing in from the ocean. The foundations of these very low cottages are almost the same as those of the Creole cottages, but the walls around the framework have been reinforced by large stones, bound together with a mix of earth and water and coated with a roughcast of lime. None of the cottages' entrances face the wind, and their few windows and doors are protected by large wooden shutters. The cottages thereby offer their occupants suitable protection from the elements.

PRACTICAL INFORMATION

Travelling throughout Saint Martin and Saint Barts is easy, whether you go by yourself or with an organized tour. In Sint Maarten (the Dutch side) the locals speak English, while French is the official language in Saint-Martin and Saint Barts. Most people working in stores, restaurants and hotels understand and speak at least a bit of English. However, there is a French-English glossary at the end of this guide, should you run into any problems. Being able to communicate is not all there is to preparing for a trip. This chapter will familiarize you with some of the local customs so that you can make the most of your vacation time.

The area code for Dutch Sint Maarten is 599.5. Changes in the telephone system oblige you to add 05.90 before every number in French Saint-Martin and Saint Barts, whether you are calling from within this area or from another French territory.

ENTRANCE FORMALITIES

Canadians, Americans and citizens of countries belonging to the EEC do not need a visa for stays of under three months. They do, however, need a passport that is valid for the length

---

Saint-Martin, Saint Martin or Sint Maarten?
Saint Barts or Saint-Barthélemy?

The use of the hyphen in "Saint-Martin" reflects the French style of hyphenation and in this guide refers to the French side of the island. "Sint Maarten" is the Dutch name for the island and refers in this guide to the Dutch side of the island. We have chosen to refer to the island as a whole as "Saint Martin".

"Saint Barts" is the English name of the French island of Saint-Barthélemy and the one used in this guide.

---

of their stay, and a return or ongoing ticket. Other travellers are admitted for three weeks.

French visitors only need their national identity card, or *carte nationale d'identité*, to enter the country.

These regulations could change at any time, and travellers are advised to check with a French or Dutch embassy or consulate before leaving.

Before leaving, ensure that you have all the required documents to enter and leave the islands. Keep these documents in a safe place during your trip. It is also a good idea to keep a photocopy of the pertinent pages of your passport, as well as your passport number and its expiry date in a separate safe place, in case the original is lost. If this should happen contact your country's embassy or consulate in order to have it replaced.

Customs

All Canadian, American, and Swiss visitors aged 17 and older are allowed onto the islands with one litre of liquor, two litres of wine and 200 cigarettes, 100 cigarillos or 250 grams of tobacco.

Citizens of legal age from member countries of the EEC are allowed 1.5 litres of spirits, four litres of wine and 300 cigarettes, 150 cigarillos or 400 grams of tobacco.

When travelling on Saint Martin between the French and Dutch territories, you will not always be aware of crossing a border because there are no official border crossings, only a simple sign marking the border. Therefore, you need not worry about customs or papers. If you decide to fly from Saint Martin to Saint Barts, you will leave from the airport in Sint Maarten, which means you wil be taking an international flight and thus will need your passport (unless you are French).

Departure Tax

The islands of Saint Martin and Saint Barts are tax free, though there is one exception for travellers. When leaving the island of Saint Martin through Princess Juliana Airport, all travellers aged two years of age and older must pay a departure tax of US$10 (120 F). Those leaving by boat must pay US$5.

The departure tax for Saint Barts is included in the airline ticket price.

PRACTICAL
INFORMATION

CONSULATES

Consulates can be an invaluable source of help to visitors who find themselves in trouble. For example, consulates can provide names of doctors or lawyers in the case of death or serious injury. However, only urgent cases are handled. It should be noted that the cost of these services is not absorbed by the consulates. There are no embassies on Saint Martin or Saint Barts; the closest consular offices to these two islands are listed below.

Australia
Consulate: Bridgetown, suite 209, 106 Saddle Road, Maraval, Box 3372, Trinidad and Tobago, ☎(809) 622-7320, ≈(809) 622-8692.

Belgium
Consulate: 1 Passe Dessart, ZI Jarry, 97152 Pointe-à-Pitre, Guadeloupe, ☎05.90.26.60.18, ⚏05.90.26.87.20.

Canada
Consulate: 72 South Quay, Box 1246, Port-of-Spain, Trinidad and Tobago, ☎(809) 623-7254 or 625-6734, ⚏(809) 624-4016.

Germany
Consulate: Box 828, Port-of-Spain, Trinidad and Tobago, ☎(809) 628-1630, ⚏(809) 628-5278.

Great Britain
High Commission: Lower Collymore Rock, Box 676, Bridgetown City, Barbados, ☎(809) 436-6694.

Netherlands
Consulate: 4446 Avenue Maurice Bishop, Fort-de-France, Martinique, ☎05.96.63.30.04, ⚏05.96.63.42.65.

Switzerland
Consulate: 21 de la Jambette, Le Lamentin, Martinique 97232, ☎05.96.50.12.43.

United States
Consulate: 14 Rue Blénac BP 561, Fort-de-France, Martinique 97206, ☎05.96.63.13.03, ⚏05.96.60.20.80.

TOURIST INFORMATION

Information on Saint-Martin
and Saint Barts Abroad

In Australia
Maison de la France: 25 Blight St., Sydney 2000,
☎(61) 2 9231 5244, ⚏(61) 2 9221 8682

In Belgium
Maison de la France: 21 Avenue de la Toison-d'Or, 1060 Brussels, ☎(32) 2.513.07.62, ⬚(32) 2 502.04.10

In Canada
Maison de la France: 1981 Avenue McGill College, Montréal, Québec H3A 2W9, ☎(514) 288-4264, ⬚(514) 845-4868.

Maison de la France: 30 St. Patrick Street, Suite 700, Toronto, Ontario M5T 3A3, ☎(416) 593-4723, ⬚(416) 979-7587.

In Germany
Maison de la France: Postfach 100128, 60325 Frankfurt a. M. ☎(49) 0190 57 00 25, ⬚(49) 0190 59 90 61.

In Great Britain
Maison de la France: 178 Piccadilly, London WIV OAL, ☎(44) 171 629-1272, ⬚(44) 171 493-6594.

In the Netherlands
Maison de la France: Prinsengracht 670, 1017 KX Amsterdam, ☎(31) 20.627.33.18, ⬚(31) 20.620.33.39.

In Switzerland
Maison de la France: 2 Rue Thalberg, 1201 Geneva, ☎(41) 22.732.86.10, ⬚(41) 22.731.58.73.

Maison de la France: Lowenstrasse 59, Postfach 7226, 8023 Zurich, ☎(41) 1.221.35.61, ⬚(41) 1.212.16.44.

In the United States
Maison de la France: 444 Madison Avenue, New York, NY 10010, ☎(212) 838-7800, ⬚(212) 838-7855.

Maison de la France: 676 North Michigan Avenue, Chicago, Illinois 60611-2819, ☎(312) 751-7800, ⬚(312) 337-6339.

Maison de la France: 9454 Wilshire Boulevard, Suite 715, Beverly Hills, California 90212-2967, ☎(310) 271-6665, ⬚(310) 276-2835.

Information on Sint Maarten Abroad

In Canada
Sint Maarten Tourist Office: 343 Ellerslie Avenue, Willowdale, Ontario M2N 1Y5, ☎(416) 223-3501.

In the United States
Sint Maarten Tourist Office: c/o Roy and P. Moss, 675 Third Avenue, Suite 2300, New York, New York 10017, ☎(212) 953-2084 or 800-786-2278.

Tourist Information in Saint Martin and Saint Barts

On Saint Barts
Quai du Général De Gaulle, Gustavia, 97095, ☎05.90.27.87.27, ⇌05.90.27.74.47, www.saint-barths.com.

In Saint-Martin
Next to Place Marché, Port de Marigot, 97150, ☎05.90.87.57.23.
There is another toruist information office on the Route de Sandy Ground
Internet: www.st-martin.org, www.frenchcaribbean.com

In Sint Maarten
St. Maarten Tourist Bureau, Imperial Building, 23 Walter Nisbeth Road, Philipsburg, ☎(5995) 22-337, ⇌(5995) 22-734, www.st-maarten.com.

GETTING TO SAINT MARTIN

The island of Saint Martin has two international airports; on the French side is L'Espérance Airport (near Grand Case), which is only equipped to receive small planes, although most travellers arrive at the Princess Juliana Airport on the Dutch side. Many people arrive on Saint Martin by boat, as many cruise ships stop here. These visitors invariably arrive on the Dutch side of the island, as the port of Philipsburg is the only one large enough to receive cruise ships.

By Plane

Princess Juliana Airport

Most visitors arriving by plane land at the Princess Juliana Airport (Dutch side), which has all the necessary facilities to welcome them: a long runway located at the end of the beach of Maho Bay, duty-free shops, restaurants and car-rental companies. This place is always busy.

General Information: ☎(599-5) 54.211
Flight information: ☎(599-5) 52.161

Several airlines have offices here:

Air Saint-Barth: ☎(599-5) 53.151
Air France: ☎(599-5) 54.212
KLM: ☎(599-5) 54.240
Winair: ☎(599-5) 52.568
AOM, Bellevue: ☎(599-5) 54.344

If you want to rent a car, several companies have counters at the airport. All are located at the airport's exit (see p 120), and they all want to rent you a car, so you can try to negotiate, although it is hard to get any deals during the high season, when things are at their busiest. It is a good idea to reserve in advance.

The airport is located 10 kilometres from Philipsburg and 8 kilometres from Marigot. One road leads to both these cities. To reach Philipsburg by car, turn right when leaving the airport. There are two possible routes for Marigot. You can take the road toward Philipsburg, where after a few kilometres you'll come to another road that cuts into the interior and leads right to Marigot. The other way is to turn left when exiting the airport towards the Terres Basses; this road leads directly to Marigot. Few vehicles take the second route, which is actually very easy.

You can also take a taxi to Marigot. Remember that taxis do not have meters, and that there are fixed rates to get around the island. For example to get from the airport to Marigot or Philipsburg costs US$8.

Finally small buses run everywhere on the island, and will get you from the airport to Philipsburg for US$1.50. Once in Philipsburg, you'll have to take another bus to Marigot (another US$1.50). Departures are about every 10 minutes.

L'Espérance Airport

L'Espérance Airport (French side) can only accommodate small planes (those serving other Caribbean islands) and is not nearly as busy as Princess Juliana. In fact, everything here closes at certain times. If you are heading to Saint Barts, it may be preferable to fly from this airport, which is less busy than the Juliana Airport on the Dutch side. The wait at the check-in desk is shorter, and the place is much calmer overall. However, this airport offers fewer services.

Flight information is available by calling ☎05.90.87.53.03.

Several airline companies have counters here:

Air Saint-Barthélemy ☎05.90.87.10.36
Air Guadeloupe: ☎05.90.87.76.59

You can also rent a car (see p 74) at the airport. Chances are you will leave the island of Saint-Martin from Princess Juliana Airport. Thus, it is wise to check if you can leave your car there, even if you rented it at L'Esperance Airport.

The airport is about one kilometre from Grand Case and five kilometres from Marigot. To get to either town, take the main road heading west.

By Boat

Several cruise lines criss-cross the Caribbean, making stop-overs in Sint Maarten. Ships like the *Princess Cruise* and the *TSS Festival* dock at the port of Philipsburg where you can shop on bustling Frontstreet or enjoy one of the beautiful beaches of the area.

GETTING TO SAINT BARTS

The island of Saint Barts only has one airport and can only handle small planes. Thus, travellers from North America or Europe will usually arrive at Sint Maarten or Guadeloupe and then change to a smaller plane. Boaters can use the port of Gustavia on Saint Barts, which is equipped to receive cruise ships despite its small size.

By Plane

Even though it is tiny, the **Saint Barts Airport** offers all the services of an international airport, including customs, car rental agencies and a small restaurant.

Travellers can get flight information by calling ☎05.90.27.65.41, or by calling the airlines directly.

The following airline companies have offices at the airport:

Air Guadeloupe: ☎05.90.27.61.90
Air Saint-Barth: ☎05.90.27.61.90
Winair: ☎05.90.27.61.01

All the car rental agencies have their offices in a building adjacent to the airport. They are set up right next to each other, offer similar prices and vehicles: basically, you have the choice between a *MOKE*, a small all-terrain vehicle with a soft top, or the more solid *Suzuki Sidekick*. It is unlikely that you will get any deals in terms of rates, especially in the high season when most cars are reserved in advance; plan ahead.

Avis: ☎05.90.27.71.43
Budget: ☎05.90.27.66.30
Europcar: ☎05.90.27.73.33
Hertz: ☎05.90.27.71.14
Island Car Rental: ☎05.90.27.62.55

PRACTICAL
INFORMATION

There are no shops in the airport. There is, however, a shopping centre in front of the airport with a bank and some shops (perfume, alcohol, etc.)

The airport is about two kilometres from Saint-Jean and Gustavia. If you have rented a car or scooter, turn left as you exit the parking lot to reach Saint-Jean, and right to reach Gustavia.

You can also take a taxi, since there is a depot at the airport. Call ☎05.90.27.75.81 to reserve one.

Finally, there is no public transportation on the island. Besides taxis or a rental cars, the only options are walking and hitchhiking.

By Boat

Several Caribbean cruise lines stop in Saint Barts. Ships like the *Sea Goddess*, the *Renaissance*, the *Star Flyer* and the *Sun Viking* dock at the port of Gustavia. From there you can shop or enjoy one of the beautiful beaches of the area.

BETWEEN SAINT MARTIN AND SAINT BARTS

If you have a free day, you might consider an excusion to Saint Martin or Saint Barts. Since the islands are only about 30 kilometres apart, many companies offer such trips. By plane or by boat, this is a great way to spend the day (especially heading from Saint Martin to Saint Barts by boat), what with the beautiful scenery and the exciting crossing.

Boats leave daily from Philipsburg (Bobby's Marina) in Sint Maarten or from the the port of Gustavia, in Saint Barts, and take about 90 minutes to make the crossing. The seas are often quite high (especially in the summer), and the trip can be rough for those with queazy stomachs (bring along some motion sickness pills). Seafaring types will find the crossing spectacular and enjoy every minute. **Gustavia Express** *(departures from l'Anse Macrel, ☎05.90.27.54.65)*, **White Octopus** *(departures from Philipsburg)*, **Voyageur** *(departures from*

Marigot and Philipsburg; Marigot ☎05.90.87.10.68, Saint Barts ☎05.90.27.54.10) and **The Edge** *(departures from Philipsburg)* are among the companies offering this trip out of Saint Martin for US$50 or US$80 with lunch and a tour of Saint Barts. Tickets are available at a stand at the entrance to Bobby's marina (Philipsburg). Out of Saint Barts, similar trips cost 270 F and are offered by **Saint-Barth Express** and **Dauphin II**.

By plane the trip takes 10 minutes, during which time a small twin-engine plane takes you for a stable ride (relatively speaking) across the ocean. Departures are from the Princess Juliana and L'Espérance airports.

There are several daily flights between the two islands, but it is nonetheless advisable to reserve in advance, particularly if you wish to leave on a particular day and time. The return trip costs approximately US$100. Air Guadeloupe, Air St. Barth and Winnair, the inter-island carriers, offer this service.

Air Guadeloupe
Marigot: ☎05.90.87.53.74
Princess Juliana Airport: ☎54-212
L'Esperance Airport: ☎05.90.87.76.59
Saint-Barts: ☎05.90.27.61.50

Air St. Barth
Princess Juliana Airport: ☎53-651
L'Esperance Airport: ☎05.90.87.10.36
Saint-Barts: ☎05.90.27.61.90

Winnair
Princess Juliana Airport: ☎52-568
Saint-Barths: ☎05.90.27.61.01

PRACTICAL
INFORMATION

INSURANCE

Cancellation Insurance

Cancellation insurance is usually offered by the travel agent when you buy your airline ticket or tour package. It allows you to be reimbursed for the ticket or trip if your vacation must be cancelled due to serious illness or death. Healthy people will probably have little need for this sort of protection, but it is always very useful to have.

Theft Insurance

Most house insurance policies in North America protect some of your goods from theft, even if the theft occurs outside the country. To make a claim, you must fill out a police report. It may not be necessary to take out further insurance, depending on the amount covered by your current house insurance policy. European visitors should ensure that their insurance policy protects their goods when they are abroad.

Life Insurance

Several airline companies offer a life insurance plan included in the price of the airplane ticket. However, many travellers already have this type of insurance and it is therefore not necessary for them to purchase more.

Health Insurance

Before leaving, it is strongly recommended that you verify that you are adequately insured in case you should become ill. It is easy to purchase health insurance before leaving. Your insurance plan should be as complete as possible because health care costs can increase rapidly in Saint Martin and Saint Barts. These islands only have small clinics, and serious injuries or illnesses are generally treated in Guadeloupe, which often results in high transportation costs. Thus, it is important to make sure your policy includes such extra costs.

When buying insurance, make sure it covers all types of medical costs, such as hospitalization, nurse's services and doctor's fees. Make sure your limit is high enough, as these fees are expensive. A repatriation clause is also a good idea in case the required care is not available on site. Furthermore, you may have to pay these costs before leaving the clinic; verify what your policy provides for in this case. During your vacation, keep proof of your insurance policy on you, so that you can avoid any problems if you need it.

HEALTH

You can rest easy in the knowledge that, no matter what happens, you will be given quality medical care when visiting Saint Martin and Saint Barts, and that the pharmacies are numerous and sell the latest medications. It is not necessary to protect yourself against any infectious diseases before travelling to Saint Martin or Saint Barts. Only those arriving from areas infected with yellow fever must be vaccinated against it.

A small **first-aid kit** can help you avoid many difficulties; prepare it carefully before leaving on your trip. Ensure that you have enough of all your regular medications, as well as a valid prescription in case you lose this supply. Other medication, such as Imodium or an equivalent, should also be bought before leaving. In addition, bring adhesive bandages, disinfectants, analgesics, antihistamines, an extra pair of glasses and pills for upset stomach.

Of course these islands are not worry-free when it comes to your health. Their two greatest attributes, the sun and the food, can also cause problems for tourists. Digestive problems, involving diarrhea and fever, do occur. If you get diarrhea, soothe your stomach by avoiding solids; instead, drink carbonated beverages, bottled water, or weak tea (avoid milk) until you recover. If the symptoms persist, see a doctor.

The **sun**'s benefits are many, but so are its harms. Always wear sunscreen (SPF 15 for adults and 25 for children) and apply it 20 to 30 minutes before exposure. Many creams on the market do not offer adequate protection; ask a pharmacist. Too much sun can cause sunstroke (dizziness, vomiting, fever, etc.). Be careful, especially the first few days, as it takes time to get used to the sun. A parasol, a hat and a pair of sunglasses are useful accessories for any day at the beach.

Insects are abundant everywhere on the island and can be quite unpleasant. They are particularly numerous during the rainy season. To minimize the chances of being bitten, cover yourself

PRACTICAL INFORMATION

well, avoid bright-coloured clothing, do not wear perfume, and use a good insect repellent. Remember, insects are more active at sundown. When walking in the mountains and forest areas, wear shoes and socks that protect your feet and legs. It is also advisable to carry ointments that will soothe the irritation caused by bites. Coil repellents will allow you to enjoy evenings on a terrace and in your room with the windows open.

You must also be careful to avoid coming into contact with the **manchineel tree**. This tree of the euphorbiacous family produces a poisonous sap that causes serious burns. It has been systematically removed from the beach areas but a few remain in certain places. Most of these have been marked by a red stripe of paint or a sign. The trees are recognizable by their small round leaves with a yellow central vein. Both the tree trunk and the leaves are dangerous, so do not touch them. Avoid using them for shelter during rain showers because the drops of rainwater carry the poisonous sap and can burn you. Furthermore, eating the fruit of this tree is also dangerous. If you do sustain a burn from this tree, or eat the fruit, consult a doctor immediately.

The water is potable throughout Saint Martin and Saint Barts.

CLIMATE

The average temperature in Saint Barts and Saint Martin is 26°C. The heat is never stifling as regular breezes and trade winds come from the east and northeast. There are, however, still two seasons; the dry season, from November to April, and the rainy season, from May to October. The dry season is the more pleasant of the two because the heat is less intense, there is less rain, and the humidity is lower. The average temperature during this season is 24°C during the day, and 19°C at night. Travelling during the rainy season is also possible because even though rain showers are heavy, they do not last long. There is more rain from August to October. This is also hurricane season. During the rainy season, expect the temperature to hover around 27°C during the day and 22°C at night. The average hours of sunshine remain constant throughout the year.

Weather forecasts are available by calling ☎05.90.90.22.22 in Saint-Martin, ☎54-226 in Sint Maarten and ☎05.90.27.60.17 in Saint Barts.

Marine forecasts are broadcast twice a day on radio station RFO (88.9 FM) at 6:28am and 6:50pm.

PACKING

The type of clothing required does not vary much from season to season. In general, loose-fitting, comfortable cotton clothes are the most useful. Closed shoes that cover the entire foot are preferred for walking in the city because they protect against cuts that might become infected. Bring a sweater or long-sleeved shirt for cool evenings, and rubber sandals to wear at the beach and in the shower. An umbrella is useful during the rainy season. Bring more dressy clothes if you anticipate evenings out. Finally, if you plan on doing some hiking, bring along appropriate footwear.

PRACTICAL INFORMATION

SAFETY

Like everywhere, there is a risk of theft in Saint Martin (less so in Saint Barts). A certain amount of caution can help preempt any potential problems. It is in your best interest to avoid taking out all your money when buying something and to leave nothing of value visible in your car.

A money belt can be used to conceal cash, traveller's cheques and your passport. That way if your bags should happen to be stolen, you will at least have money and the necessary documents to help you out. Remember that the less attention you draw to yourself, the less chance you have of being robbed.

If you bring valuables to the beach, be sure to keep a constant eye on them. It is safer to keep your valuables in the small safes available at most hotels.

GETTING AROUND THE ISLANDS

Saint Martin's road network is easy to sum up: basically one road skirts the island, and another one links Marigot and Philipsburg. There are also a few smaller roads, sometimes unpaved, that lead to some of the beaches. Relatively few cars travel these thruways, but traffic is nevertheless often heavy at the entrance to Philipsburg. The speed limit is usually 90 kph on these roads (110 kph in certain places).

Saint Barts, with its 25 square kilometres of terrain, has a limited road network that is nonetheless quite sufficient for its inhabitants. There is little traffic on the roads, most of which are paved (except a few roads leading to quieter beaches), and often narrow and bumpy. Getting around by car is very easy.

Driving Tips

It is easy to find your way around the islands. Signs are generally clear and reliable, so reaching the centre of all the towns and villages is not a problem, although some areas in the Dutch half of Saint Martin are not as well signed out.

Most roads are not well lit and often wind their way through hills, so be careful when driving at night.

Do not forget that you must give right of way to traffic coming from the right. This means that at intersections, you must yield to the car on the right no matter who got there first.

Be careful when approaching speed bumps, especially on Saint Martin, where they have been placed on the outskirts of towns and near resort areas. They are usually well marked, and most are painted yellow. Some, however, are poorly marked. To avoid any unpleasant surprises, slow down when travelling through towns especially near the touristy areas like Baie Nettlé and Mullet Bay.

To make travelling throughout the islands easier, buy the IGN (*Institut Géographique National*) map of Guadeloupe, with a

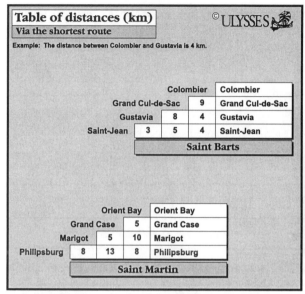

Table of distances (km)
Via the shortest route

©ULYSSES

Example: The distance between Colombier and Gustavia is 4 km.

			Colombier	Colombier
		Grand Cul-de-Sac	9	Grand Cul-de-Sac
	Gustavia		8	4	Gustavia
	Saint-Jean	3	5	4	Saint-Jean

Saint Barts

		Orient Bay	Orient Bay
	Grand Case	5	Grand Case
Marigot	5	10	Marigot
Philipsburg	8	13	8	Philipsburg

Saint Martin

1:100,000 scale. There is also a more precise map of Saint Martin and Saint Barts with a 1:25,000 scale.

There are gas stations throughout Saint Martin. The price of gas is about on par with average North American prices, a little less expensive on Saint Barts. Most stations accept credit cards.

Renting a Car

There are car-rental agencies in the Princess Juliana, L'Espérance and Saint Barts airports, as well as in most resort areas. Wherever you go, you can expect to pay about US$60 for an economy car and US$80 or more for an all-terrain vehicle (unlimited mileage) per day, not counting insurance and taxes.

In Saint Barts, most agencies rent the same two types of vehicles: all-terrain types (Suzukis) or MOKEs, cute little topless cars that are perfect for drives along the coast. Expect to pay at least 300 F per day during the high season.

When renting a car, it is recommended that you take out automobile insurance to cover all costs in case of an accident. If you are paying by credit card, don't forget that certain gold cards offer automatic accident insurance if you use them to pay for your rental car. Before signing the contract, make sure that payment details are clearly defined. Your credit card must be able to cover the rental costs as well as the insurance deductible when you sign the contract.

A valid drivers' license from your home country is acceptable.

You must be 21 years of age to rent a car.

If you are travelling during the busy season, make sure to reserve your vehicle in advance.

Renting a Bicycle or a Scooter

If the open road beckons, it is easy to rent a motorcycle, a scooter or a bicycle. A scooter costs approximately 150 F per day and a bicycle costs 60 F per day. You will need to leave your drivers' license as a deposit, as well as 300 F when renting a scooter. Remember to always drive carefully, and that wearing a helmet is obligatory. Saint Martin's sunny roads and Saint Barts' steep hills might discourage more leisurely cyclists.

Saint Martin

Marigot

Eugène Moto: ☎05.90.87.13.97

Baie Nettlé

Rent a Scoot: ☎05.90.87.20.59

Saint Barts

Gustavia

Chez Béranger: ☎05.90.27.89.00
Fredo Moto: Rue Courbet

Saint-Jean

Ouanalao Moto Galeries du Commerce (next to the airport): ☎05.90.27.88.74

Taxis

Taxis are one of the most efficient ways of getting around Saint Martin. No meters are used, and all the rates are fixed (and non-negotiable, by the way). Here are a few sample rates:

Marigot - Baie Nettlé	US$10
Marigot -Grand Case	US$8
Marigot - L'Espérance airport	US$8
Marigot - Oyster Pond	US$20
Marigot - Philipsburg	US$8
Philipsburg - Orient Bay	US$15
Philipsburg - Mullet Bay	US$8
Princess Juliana airport- Baie Nettlé	US$15

On Saint Barts, taxis can be found near the marina in Gustavia and next to the airport in Saint-Jean. You can also get one by calling:

Gustavia: ☎05.90.27.66.31
Airport: ☎05.90.27.75.81

Buses

There is no public transportation system on Saint Martin. The buses that traverse the island are run by several private operations, and they do not serve the whole island. For example, there is no bus to Terres Basses. Essentially these buses are good to get from Mullet Bay to Philipsburg, from

Philipsburg to Orient Bay, from Philipsburg to Marigot, and from Marigot to Grand Case. It is an efficient and inexpensive way to get around (as long as you want to get to one of these places). The buses are identified by small signs in their windshields that list the places they stop.

There are no buses on Saint Barts.

Hitchhiking

For many locals, hitchhiking is the easiest way to get around (especially between cities not served by buses). When travelling short distances, people will often hitch a ride while waiting for a bus (just in case). This usually works well. However, a certain degree of caution is advised for women travelling alone.

Hitchhiking is also an option in Saint Barts. Remember, however, that in certain areas, cars pass very infrequently and it can be faster to walk since distances are short.

MONEY AND BANKING

Three different currencies can be used on Saint Martin: the American dollar, the French franc, and the Dutch guilder. Francs are only accepted on the French side, and guilders only on the Dutch side (pretty strange on an island that for the most part does not have a border-crossing). So don't try to pay in francs in Philipsburg or in guilders at L'Espérance. If you are staying only in the Dutch zone, bring only American dollars instead of worrying about two currencies. However, if you are staying in Saint-Martin you have the choice between francs or American dollars. Wherever you stay, bring some of both currencies in case you decide to visit the other side, and remember that the international airport is in Sint Maarten.

For certain foreign travellers, notably Canadians, it may be more profitable to pay in francs than in US dollars (depending on the exchange rate, of course). It is thus a good idea to check the exchange rates each time you change money.

The French franc is the official currency on Saint Barts, but several merchants also accept American dollars.

The prices given in this guide are in US dollars for Sint Maarten and in French francs for Saint-Martin and Saint Barts.

Banks

On Saint Martin, most banks can exchange foreign currencies into francs, guilders and American dollars. They usually offer good rates. In Sint Maarten banks are open for transactions Monday to Thursday from 8:30am to 3:30pm, and until 4:30pm Friday. The bank at Princess Juliana airport is open every day from 8:30am to 5:30pm. In Saint-Martin, banks are open from 8am to noon and 2pm to 4pm.

On Saint Barts, there are banks near the airport and in Gustavia. All of them can change foreign currencies into francs or American dollars. They are generally open from Monday to Friday, from 8am to noon and 1pm to 5pm.

Banks close at noon the day before legal holidays on both islands.

Most bank machines accept Visa and MasterCard for cash advances; North Americans with automated teller machine bank cards that work with the Cirrus, Interac or PLUS systems can also withdraw money from instant tellers at any time. These machines can be found in a few cities, in particular Pointe-à-Pitre, Gosier and Saint-François. It is the fastest and easiest way to withdraw money, which is given to you in French francs. Service charges are usually withdrawn from your account for each transaction, but the exchange rates usually prove to be a little better.

Currency Exchange

You can also change your money at currency exchange offices. The rates are sometimes not as good, but there is no commission charged.

PRACTICAL INFORMATION

Exchange Rates

US$1	=	$1.47 CAN	$1 CAN	=	US$0.68
US$1	=	0.97 EURO	1 EURO	=	US$1.03
US$1	=	£ 0.63	£ 1	=	US1.59
US$1	=	$1.53 Aust	$1 Aust	=	US$0.65
US$1	=	$1.88 NZ	$1 NZ	=	US$0.53
US$1	=	1.89 DM	1 DM	=	US$0.53
US$1	=	2.13 guilder	1 guilder	=	US$0.47
US$1	=	39.06 BF	10 BF	=	US$0.26
US$1	=	1.54 SF	1 SF	=	US$0.65
US$1	=	161.12 peseta	100 peseta	=	US$0.62
US$1	=	1,874.969 lira	1000 lira	=	US$0.53
1 FF	=	$0.23 CAN	$1 CAN	=	4.32 FF
1 FF	=	$0.16 US	$1 US	=	6.34 FF
1 FF	=	0.15 EURO	1 EURO	=	6.56 FF
1 FF	=	£ 0.10	£ 1	=	10.11 FF
1 FF	=	$0.24 Aust	$1 Aust	=	4.16 FF
1 FF	=	$0. 30 NZ	$1 NZ	=	3.38 FF
1 FF	=	0.30 DM	1 DM	=	3.35 FF
1 FF	=	0.34 guilder	1 guilder	=	2.98 FF
1 FF	=	6.15 BF	10 BF	=	1.63 FF
1 FF	=	0.24 SF	1 SF	=	4.11 FF
1 FF	=	25.36 peseta	100 peseta	=	3.94 FF
1 FF	=	295.07 lira	1000 lira	=	3.39 FF

Large hotels also change money. However, rates are worse than at banks or currency exchange offices.

Traveller's Cheques

It is always best to keep most of your money in traveller's cheques. Get your cheques in US dollars if you will be visiting Sint Maarten, and in French francs if you will be visiting Saint-Martin or Saint Barts. Always keep a copy of the serial numbers of your cheques separate from the cheques, in case they are lost, so that the company can easily and quickly cancel the old cheques and replace them.

Credit Cards

Credit cards, especially Visa (Carte Bleue) and MasterCard, are accepted by most businesses. However, do not count on using them everywhere, and always make sure you have some cash with you. In Saint-Martin, on the French side, you may be surprised to note that the bill sometimes comes in US dollars rather than francs. The reason for this is very simple: merchants often do business with banks on the Dutch side. Certain travellers may find it less advantageous to pay in US dollars than in francs and should thus always request that prices be set in the currency of their choice, an option that is sometimes feasible.

Cheques

French visitors should not count on paying with personal cheques, since many businesses do not accept them because of the risk of fraud.

MAIL AND TELECOMMUNICATIONS

Telecommunications offices from which you can make long-distance calls can be found in Marigot, Philipsburg and Gustavia.

These offices also sell phone cards to be used in public telephone booths. These cards come in two denominations in Saint-Martin: 36 F and 87 F. In Sint Maarten there is only one, which costs US$9.95.

The area code for Dutch Sint Maarten is 599.5. Changes in the telephone system oblige you to add 05.90 before every number in French Saint-Martin and Saint Barts, whether you are calling from within this area or from another French territory. From anywhere else, dial 590.

To phone from Saint-Martin
To phone Sint Maarten dial 00 + 599-5 + the 5-digit phone number.

PRACTICAL INFORMATION

Emergency Telephone Numbers

Saint-Martin	Ambulance: ☎05.90.87.74.14
	Hospital: ☎05.90.87.50.07
	Police: ☎05.90.87.50.04
Sint Maarten	Ambulance: ☎13-011
	Hospital: ☎31-111
	Police: ☎22-222
Saint Barts	Ambulance or Fire: ☎05.90.27.66.13
	Police: ☎05.90.27.66.66

To phone Saint Barts dial the 10-digit phone number.

To phone from Sint Maarten
To phone Saint-Martin or Saint Barts dial 00 + 590 + the 6-digit phone number.

To phone from Saint Barts
To phone Sint Maarten dial 00 + 599-5 + the 5-digit phone number.
To phone Saint-Martin dial the 10-digit phone number.

There are two ways to call long distance from the islands. The first option is to place a **direct-dial call**, which is charged according to local telephone rates. To call North America, dial 00, then 1, then the area code and the phone number.

To call overseas, dial 00, the country code (see below), then the telephone number.

Country Codes
Great Britain: 44
Netherlands: 31
Australia: 61
New Zealand: 64
Belgium: 32
Italy: 39
Switzerland: 41
Germany: 49
Canada: 01

The second option for calling long distance from the islands is to use the operator and pay the rates of the country which you are calling. The following access numbers will connect you with operators in your home country:

Canada Direct: 0-800-99-00-16

AT&T Direct: 0-800-99-00-11 (from French Saint-Martin and Saint Barts); 001-800-872-2881 (from Dutch Sint Maarten)
MCI Direct: 0-800-99-00-19 (from French Saint-Martin and Saint Barts); 001-800-888-8000 (from Dutch Sint Maarten)

Post offices have fax and telex machines.

PRACTICAL INFORMATION

Time Sharing

While strolling on the island of Saint-Martin, particularly the Dutch side, you will undoubtedly notice a few places that resemble hotel complexes but have a sign that says "private club". Though they are indeed private, you will be invited to visit one of these places on more than one occasion during a simple jaunt to Marigot or Philipsburg. These clubs, in fact, offer an innovative accommodation formula: the time-share option. If you agree to visit them you will be "treated" to — or sometimes actually pressured into attending — a sales-pitch session during which you will be offered not the outright purchase of a flat, but simply to "own" it for one week per year. Love it or hate it, the fact remains that there are dozens of these complexes on the island. If you are not interested, refuse any invitation and abstain from participating in any contest entitling you to attend. Note, however, that you can sometimes lease one of these apartments without being a member; simply inquire within.

ACCOMMODATIONS

Luxurious and comfortable hotels abound on Saint Martin and Saint Barts. Staying on the cheap, however, can be quite a challenge. The *Association des Gîtes de France*, a French bed and breakfast association, does not have any members on the island, and there are very few "budget hotels".

We have listed what we believe to be the best accommodations, keeping in mind the price category, location and particular advantages of each one. Prices indicated were valid at press time, and apply to a standard room for two people during the high season (January to April). They are of course subject to change at any time. For Saint-Martin and Sint Maarten, a **five percent tax** is added to the rates cited in this guide. Saint Barts, of course, is tax-free (see p 31).

RESTAURANTS

Excellent restaurants of all kinds are certainly not what's missing on the island of Saint Martin, especially on the French side. From small French bistros to restaurants serving refined French cuisine or exotic specialties, not to mention the little food stands along the beach specializing in seafood and grilled fish, there is a spot to suit everyone's taste.

Meanwhile, Saint Barts has several fine dining establishments, pleasant bistros that serve French and Creole dishes, and cafés where you can stop in for a sandwich or some ice cream. Whatever your tastes, you will eat well on either island!

In an effort to satisfy the needs of all our readers, we have sampled and tasted throughout the island in order to offer a selection of restaurants for all budgets. A phone number and address is included for each establishment, where possible. **The price indicated is the price of a meal for one person including tip, but excluding drinks.**

HOLIDAYS

All banks and several businesses are closed on public holidays. Be sure to change money and do your shopping the day before.

In the following list (F) indicates a holiday on the French side, and (D) a holiday on the Dutch side.

January 1 (F/D)	New Year's Day
Variable (F)	Shrove Tuesday (*Mardi Gras*)
Variable (F/D)	Ash Wednesday
Variable (F/D)	Easter Sunday and Monday
April 30 (D)	Queen's birthday
May 1 (F/D)	Labour Day
May 8 (F)	Remembrance Day Armistice 1945
Variable (F/D)	Ascension Day
May 27 (F)	Abolition of Slavery
Variable (F)	Whitsun
July 14 (F)	National Holiday
July 21 (F)	Victor Schœchler Day
August 15 (F)	Assumption
August 24 (F)	Fête de Saint-Barthélemy (Saint Barts)
November 1 (F)	All Saints' Day
November 11 (F)	Remembrance Day Armistice 1918
November 11 (D/F)	Saint Martin Day
December 25 (F/D)	Christmas

PRACTICAL
INFORMATION

CALENDAR OF EVENTS

Various festivals are celebrated throughout the year, with parades, dancing, music and games of all sorts. Below is a list of some of the more noteworthy events.

● Saint Barts' week-long international music festival has been held every January for more than ten years.

● Carnival is celebrated on both islands but at different times, leading to double the fun. In French Saint-Martin and Saint Barts, it starts a few day before Shrove Tuesday (*Mardi Gras*) and ends on Ash Wednesday (*Mercredi des Cendres*) when the carnival effigy is burned. In Dutch Sint Maarten, the carnival takes place during the last two weeks of April. Among the activities are the elections of a Carnival queen and a Calypso king.

● The waters off Sint Maarten fill with colourful yachts for the Heineken regattas in March.

• July 14 is the French national holiday and a time for parades, sports competitions and fireworks, both in Saint-Martin and Saint Barts.

• Schœlcher day, which commemorates the emancipation of the slaves, is celebrated on July 21 in Grand Case.

• The Fête de Saint-Barthélemy takes place on August 24 and is a perfect opportunity to celebrate and organise regattas, games and races. The next day, August 25, Saint Louis is celebrated in Corossol.

• November 11 sees parties throughout the island of Saint Martin to mark Saint Martin Day.

MISCELLANEOUS

Electricity

As in continental Europe, appliances work on 220 Volts (50 cycles). Even though there are a few 110-Volt plugs, North Americans should bring along a converter and an adapter.

Women Travellers

Women travelling to these islands don't need to worry: life is peaceful and violence is infrequent. Of course, the usual amount of caution should be exercised.

Time Difference

Saint Barts and Saint Martin are on Eastern Standard Time. However, there is no daylight savings time, so in winter the islands are one hour ahead of Montréal and New York. There is five hours difference between the islands and Greenwich Mean Time during the summer and four hours in the winter.

Accommodations on Saint Martin, such as this one,
are each more lavish than the last. - *L.P.*

Some pristine white sand beaches with turquoise waters remain on Saint Martin.
- *L.P.*

Dolls clothed in madras, a traditional Antillean fabric, are sold at the market in Marigot.
- *L.P.*

Weights and Measures

Both islands use the metric system. Here are a few equivalencies.

Weights
1 pound (lb) = 454 grams (g)
1 kilogram (kg) = 2.2 pounds (lbs)

Linear Measure
1 inch = 2.2 centimetres (cm)
1 foot (ft) = 30 centimetres (cm)
1 mile = 1.6 kilometres (km)
1 kilometre (km) = 0.63 miles
1 metre (m) = 39.37 inches

Land Measure
1 acre = 0.4 hectare (ha)
1 hectare (ha) = 2.471 acres

Volume Measure
1 U.S. gallon (gal) = 3.79 litres
1 U.S. gallon (gal) = 0.83 imperial gallon

Temperature
To convert °F into °C: subtract 32, divide by 9, multiply by 5
To convert °C into °F: multiply by 9, divide by 5, add 32.

OUTDOORS

W hether you want to ride the waves, discover underwater treasures or relish the beach from under the shade of a beach parasol, the islands of Saint-Martin and Saint Barts are sure to please. And while the beaches of the former are among the prettiest in the Lesser Antilles, the latter will charm you with its lovely and quiet coves. Whatever your sport or activity, a little preparation will go a long way toward helping you make the most of your excursions.

 SWIMMING

Ahhh, the sea... crystal-clear, refreshing waters, waves perfect for all types of activities: an integral part of any vacation. Remember, though, that the better one understands the sea, the better one is able to enjoy it. More specifically, beaches on their leeward side (Caribbean Sea) are less exposed to the wind, so the waters are much calmer; these are perfect spots for family swimming. Beaches on the windward side (Atlantic Ocean) are rougher and will please visitors in search of big waves.

A Fragile Ecosystem

Coral reefs are formed by minuscule organisms called coelenterate polyps, which are very sensitive to water pollution. The high level of nitrates in polluted water accelerate the growth of seaweed, which in turn takes over the coral, stops it from growing and literally smothers it. Sea urchins (whose long spikes can cause severe injuries) live on the coral and play a major role in controlling the amount of seaweed that grows on the coral by eating what the fish cannot. An epidemic threatened the survival of many reefs in 1983, when the waters became so polluted that sea urchins were affected and seaweed flourished in the Caribbean Sea. Scientific studies have since proved the importance of urchins to the ecological balance, and the species has thus been restored on certain reefs. However, these little urchins cannot solve the problem on their own. Pollution control is essential if the coral reefs, upon which 400,000 organisms depend, are to survive.

There are no private beaches on either Saint-Martin or Saint Barts, so you can swim anywhere you like. However, certain beaches are difficult to access because they lie behind the property of huge hotel complexes that do not allow the public onto their grounds. Nothing stops you from frequenting these beaches, just remember that most of the hotel facilities adjoining them are reserved for hotel guests, so try to stick to the beach.

 SCUBA DIVING

There are many diving centres throughout the islands offering divers the chance to explore the ocean floor surrounding Saint-Martin and Saint Barts. Certified divers can explore the secrets of these coastlines to their heart's content. Novices can also embark on underwater explorations, but must be accompanied by a qualified guide who will supervise their descent (to a maximum depth of 5 m). The sport is not dangerous; just be sure that the supervision is adequate. Before taking your first plunge, it is very important to at least take an introductory course in order to learn basic safety skills: how to clear the water from your mask, how to equalize the pressure in your ears and sinuses, how to breathe underwater (don't hold your breath) and become comfortable with the change in pressure underwater, and to familiarize yourself with the equipment. Many hotels offer a resort course of about one hour before taking first-timers under water. Equipment can easily be rented from the different centres along the coasts.

Scuba diving lets you discover fascinating sights like coral reefs, schools of multi-coloured fish and amazing underwater plants. Don't forget that this ecosystem is fragile and deserves special attention. All divers must respect a few basic **guidelines** in order to protect these natural sites: do not touch anything (especially not urchins, as their long spikes can cause injury); do not break off pieces of coral (it is much prettier in the water than on land, where it becomes discoloured); do not disturb any living creatures; do not hunt; do not feed the fish; be careful not to disturb anything with your fins and, of course, do not litter. If you want a souvenir of your underwater experience, disposable underwater cameras are available.

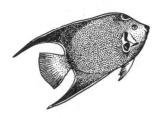

Angelfish

  SNORKELLING

If you are drawn to the sea, but not interested in diving, snorkelling is the perfect alternative. It doesn't take much to snorkel: a mask, a snorkel and some fins. Anyone can enjoy

OUTDOORS

this activity, which is a great way to appreciate the richness of the underwater world. Not far from several beaches, you can go snorkelling around coral reefs inhabited by various underwater species. Some companies organize snorkelling trips. Remember that the basic rules for protecting the underwater environment (see scuba diving section) must also be respected when snorkelling.

PARASAILING

Another unusual way to enjoy the vast expanse of the ocean is to view it from the skies, by parasailing! Securely attached to your parachute and tied to a powerful motorboat, you are hoisted up into the air in seconds. Once airborne, you have ten minutes or so to enjoy the spectacular bird's eye view of your surroundings. Not for the faint of heart.

WINDSURFING

Several of the islands' beaches are washed by calm waves, which might not suit seasoned sailboarders, but are ideal for the less experienced. The only beach on the islands that has some serious wind and waves for windsurfing is the one at the **Baie de l'Embouchure**. Less experienced boarders can enjoy practising in more controlled conditions at other locations.

DEEP-SEA FISHING

Deep-sea fishing excursions offer the excitement of a big catch on the high seas, and make for a fun outing besides. These trips usually last half a day. Equipment and fishing tips are provided by the organizers.

JET SKIING

These high-speed contraptions that fly across the water provide thrills and hours of entertainment for many travellers. Learning to manoeuver them takes little time, and reasonable caution should be exercised at all times to avoid an accident. If you are careening about, always yield the right of way to slower and less easily manoeuvrable boats (sailboats, pedal-boats, etc.), and watch out for swimmers and divers. The latter are often hard to spot, but the boat accompanying them always flies a red flag with a white line through it when the divers are down. Never approach these boats when this flag is flying.

 HIKING

Though the islands are tiny and do not have any national parks, you can still head off on foot, along the hills of Saint Barts (there is only one trail, in the **Colombier** region) or up to the top of **Pic Paradis** (400 m) on Saint-Martin. These hiking trips hold many surprises, but require some preparation in order to avoid problems associated with the hot tropical sun (see below). And though the distances are short, it is a good idea to know the level of difficulty and change of altitude of the trail you plan on hiking and to stick to the trail.

Sunstroke

Long sections of exposed trail mean that all hikers run the risk of sunstroke. Dizziness, nausea, cramps and goose bumps are the first symptoms of sunstroke. Anyone experiencing these symptoms needs immediate shade, water and ventilation. To avoid the problem, always wear a hat and a good sunscreen. By getting an early start, you'll have time for a day hike in cooler temperatures.

Clothing

The general rule is to wear lightweight and light-coloured clothing. Thick-soled shoes that are lightweight and solid with good traction are the best. Also, bring a raincoat to keep you dry in case of rain and a hat against the sun.

What to Bring?

A daypack with a pocket knife, antiseptic, bandages, adhesive bandages, scissors, aspirin, sunscreen, insecticide, food and above all enough water for the trip should be brought on every hike, regardless of the duration.

 BICYCLING

The steep, hilly and sunny roads of Saint-Martin and Saint Barts are not ideal for leisurely bike rides. There are, however, several smaller roads that lead to the islands' beaches, so short rides are possible. Bikes can be rented at different points around the island. Expect to pay about 60 F per day (see p 54).

 HORSEBACK RIDING

Saint-Martin and Saint Barts have a few riding stables that organize excursions for enthusiasts of this sport, offering a pleasant way to discover the island.

 GOLF

There is only one golf course on the island of Saint-Martin, at **Mullet Bay**. Unfortunately, most of its facilities, including the buildings of the Mullet Bay Casino and Resort, were severely damaged by Hurricane Luis in 1995. Though repairs have been made and it has reopened to golfers, the terrain remains in a sad state. The buildings are supposed to be redone, but no date has been given. There are no golf courses on Saint Barts.

FRENCH
SAINT-MARTIN

 S aint Martin's mere 55 square kilometres of French
territory comprise a large and elegant town; Marigot,
a city which abounds in seaside terraces and opulent
boutiques. Saint-Martin also has a few charming and authentic
villages, such as Grand Case, which have managed to combine
Creole life with a holiday ambiance. Between its towns and
villages, the coasts are punctuated with long crescents of blond
sand – wonderful, relaxing spots in which to savour the hot
rays of the sun and enjoy a multitude of water sports.

FINDING YOUR WAY AROUND

By Car

A single main road, in very good condition, runs through the
whole French part of the island. From Marigot, this road travels
east to Orient Bay, passing through Grand Case on the way.
Heading west, the same road goes through Terres Basses,
making its way to Sint Maarten, the Dutch part of Saint Martin.
By taking this road, travellers will easily reach the L'Esperance
airport in Grand Case to the east, or the Princess Juliana airport
to the west.

A section of road running inland also links Marigot to Philipsburg. To take this road from Marigot's downtown area, you must follow Rue de Hollande to the junction with the main road, which leads toward Philipsburg.

A few secondary roads, most of which are well paved, go to villages and isolated beaches such as Anse Marcel and Friar's Bay.

Road signs are clear and reliable.

Renting a Car

L'Espérance Airport

Avis: ☎05.90.87.50.60
Hertz: ☎05.90.87.73.01
Sanaco Car Rental: ☎05.90.87.14.93

Marigot

Avis: ☎05.90.87.50.60, www.avis.com
Eurocar: ☎05.90.27.32.80
Hertz: ☎05.90.87.40.68, ≈05.90.87.75.47
National Rent a Car: ☎05.90.27.32.80, ≈05.90.87.55.23
Island Trans Rent a Car: ☎05.90.87.91.32, ≈05.90.87.70.87

Baie Nettlé

Budget: ☎05.90.87.21.91
Hertz: ☎05.90.87.33.71

Bus Stations

Marigot: corner of Rue Président Kennedy and Rue de Hollande.

Grand Case: You can catch a bus to Marigot on the main road downtown, or right on the main road at the city's entrance.

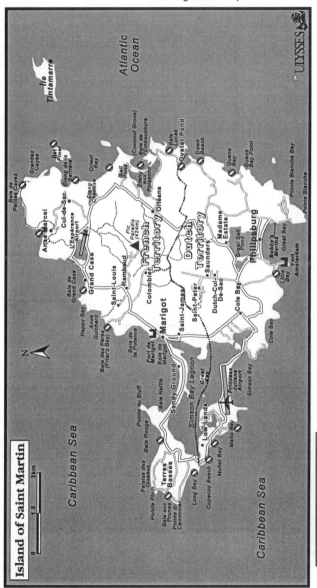

Island of Saint Martin

Taxi

For taxis, call ☎05.90.87.56.54.

 PRACTICAL INFORMATION

Tourist Information

Port de Marigot: 97150 Marigot, ☎05.90.87.57.23, ⌐05.90.87.56.43.

Banks

Banque Commerciale Française: ☎05.90.87.53.80

Banque des Antilles Françaises: Rue de la République, Marigot, ☎05.90.29.13.30.

Exchange Bureaus

Change Point: Rue du Président Kennedy, Marigot, ☎05.90.87.24.85

Change Plus: 15 Rue de la Mairie, ☎05.90.87.30.

Inter Change: Rue du Général de Gaulle, Marigot, ☎05.90.87.73.41

Post Office

Saint-Martin has post offices in Marigot, Grand Case and Baie Nettlé. If you do not wish to go all the way there, note that certain hotels also offer mail service.

Mon to Fri 7:30am to 4pm, Sat 7:30am to 11:30am

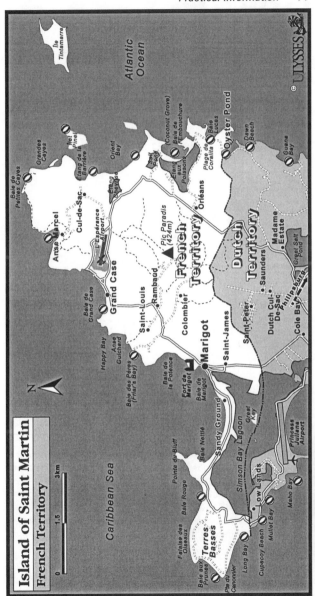

Marigot: Rue de la Liberté, ☎05.90.87.53.17

Grand Case: Boulevard Laurence, ☎05.90.87.05.96

Medical Care

Hospital

Marigot Hospital: ☎05.90.29.57.57

Ambulance

Day: ☎05.90.87.86.25
Night: ☎05.90.87.72.00

Pharmacies

Pharmacie du Port: Rue de la Liberté, Marigot, ☎05.90.87.50.79.

Pharmacie La Lagune: Résidence La Lagune, Baie Nettlé, ☎05.90.87.20.00.

Pharmacie de Grand Case: Route de la Déviation, Grand Case, ☎05.90.87.77.46.

  SIGHTS AND BEACHES

The towns and villages of Saint-Martin are certainly charming enough to hold anyone's attention, and a visit to the most beautiful among them is highly recommended. This Caribbean island's main attraction, however, is its beaches; long golden crescents of sand, bordered by azure waters, are strewn all along the coast. From Marigot, a tour through this French land, its villages and natural treasures will offer visitors an incomparable experience.

Marigot

Marigot ★★, the main town in Saint-Martin, is located on the north shore of the island, on a point of land that was one of the first areas to be colonized, thanks to its proximity to a large bay. Baie de Marigot is protected from strong winds, making it perfect for mooring boats. Though the site was advantageous for sailors, it did pose a few problems for colonists, since the Baie de Marigot was not always rimmed with sand as it is today. Originally, it was surrounded by mangroves and swampland, hence its name, which means "backwater" in French. This vegetation proved a real nuisance for colonists, who could neither cultivate nor pass through this area. They were forced to eliminate it in order to access the waters of the bay more easily.

Nature was not the only concern of the colonists of Marigot; right from the beginning, the village had to contend with attacks by the English. Starting in 1666, French authorities contemplated building a fort in order to protect the colony. It was not until 1767, however, that construction of **Fort Saint-Louis ★★** *(free admission; reached by following Rue de l'Église)* began. The project was conceived by the Chevalier Descoudrelles, a knight who sought to take advantage of the hills surrounding the bay. The fort was built on the summit of these hills and commands a full view of the bay. Construction was finished in 1789 under Descoudrelles' successor, Durat. A few years later, in 1794, the English troops conquered the magnificent, strategically placed stone structure. The fort remained in their possession until the island was liberated a few years later by Victor Hugues (see p 26). After the Treaty of Vienna (1815), the English attacks ceased and the fort was gradually abandoned. Today, its ruins still dominate the city. Visitors can tour the site and enjoy the superb **view ★** from on high.

The city of Marigot consists of a lower and an upper part. Visitors touring the lower part of the city can explore the developed area around the fort or take a leisurely tour of the hillside, with its lovely Creole cottages and beautiful colonial homes with elaborate balconies. The town has experienced gradual expansion and new districts have developed, first to

SAINT-MARTIN

the east of the fort (a high school was built), then around the ocean, in an area once covered by an insalubrious swamp that was filled around 1965. Today, visitors will see the beautiful Port la Royale marina here, as well as modern buildings housing boutiques and restaurants. All this makes the place ideal for enjoying a bite to eat while observing the comings and goings of boats, whose lovely colours brighten the horizon.

Between the fort and the Port la Royale marina is Marigot's downtown area, which occupies the area between Rue du Général de Gaulle and the outskirts of Baie de Marigot. This is where the majority of boutiques and restaurants are located, and visitors are sure to be charmed by the peaceful activity reigning throughout. A stroll through the streets of downtown should lead you to the edge of the bay, where you can spend hours contemplating the beautiful spectacle of the shimmering waves while sitting on a park bench or at a table on one of the inviting terraces, judiciously set up on this spot.

There is a large square facing this seafront where a **public market** ★ is held every Wednesday and Saturday morning. Stalls move in and take over the area, proffering all sorts of goods, from spices to fragrant exotic fruits to cotton clothing and, of course, Creole crafts. Take the time to rummage and poke about for there are sure to be a few items to please you among this jumbled pile of merchandise. A feast for the eyes, this market will delight even those who do not wish to purchase anything.

The upper part of the city extends over the west side of Marigot's hill, where the residential district of Saint-James stands, set back from the town and isolated due to its dense vegetation.

To leave Marigot, take Rue de la Liberté, which becomes the island's main road.

A museum has opened its doors next to Marigot: **Sur les Traces des Arawaks** ★★ *(US$5; 9am to noon and 3pm to 7pm, closed on Sun; ☎05.90.29.22.84).* This museum recounts the history of the island's very first inhabitants, the indigenous Arawak-speaking peoples who arrived here over 3,500 years ago. Several pieces, notably seashell tools, pottery shards and mother-of-pearl jewellery, discovered during archaeological digs

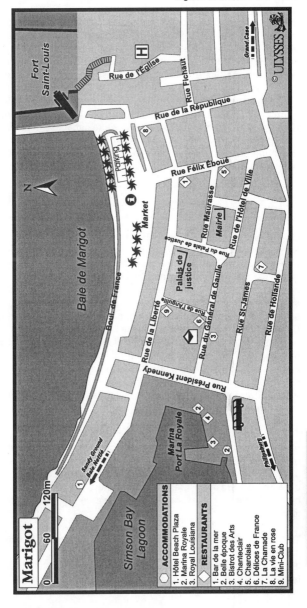

Marigot

0   60   120m

Fort Saint-Louis

Baie de Marigot

Simson Bay Lagoon

N

Boul. de France

Rue de l'Église

Rue Fichaut

Rue de la République

Rue Félix Éboué

Rue Maurasse

Rue de l'Hôtel de Ville

Rue du Palais de Justice

Rue de la Liberté

Rue du Général de Gaulle

Rue de l'Anguille

Rue St-James

Rue Hollande

Rue Président Kennedy

Parking

Market

Palais de justice

Mairie

Marina Port La Royale

Sandy Ground
Baie Nettlé

Grand Case

Philipsburg

© ULYSSES

◯ ACCOMMODATIONS
1. Hôtel Beach Plaza
2. Marina Royale
3. Royal Louisiana

◇ RESTAURANTS
1. Bar de la mer
2. Belle époque
3. Bistrot des Arts
4. Chanteclair
5. Charolais
6. Délices de France
7. La Chamade
8. La vie en rose
9. Mini-Club

SAINT-MARTIN

executed on the island, are exhibited. Each object is accompanied by a host of information about these people, allowing visitors to better understand their way of life and their beliefs. Museums dedicated to the Arawaks are rare, so this is a good opportunity to learn more about these people who were destroyed following the arrival of the first European colonists. A second room presents the life of the inhabitants of Saint Martin at the turn of the century. This fascinating trip through time is illustrated with black-and-white images depicting everyday scenes from that era and these photographs are all the more interesting as they are often paired with others portraying the same scene today.

Terres Basses

On the way out of Marigot, heading west, you'll arrive at **Sandy Ground**, which is actually an extension of the city. A few restaurants and beaches make up the bulk of this hamlet, which is the gateway to the **Terres Basses**, or lowlands, a narrow strip of land in the shape of a loop leading to the Dutch side of the island. Several tourist villages have been constructed on these lowlands, where one shore gives onto the Caribbean Sea and the other onto the Simson Bay Lagoon. One of these is located at **Baie Nettlé**, alongside some stunning **beaches** ★. Some of the most beautiful hotel complexes on the French side of the island are found here (see p 96). Each comprises comfortable buildings, housing both rooms and restaurants. Things are much quieter in these isolated establishments than in the village of Mullet Bay.

This part of the island is sparsely inhabited, save for these tourist areas and a scattering of opulent residences that stand high in the hills enabling their residents to enjoy superb views out over the crystalline waters of the sea. These houses can only be admired from afar, but no matter: the big attraction here is the beautiful beaches, which are among the best on the island.

The first beach you'll encounter coming from Marigot is the one at **Baie Rouge** ★★. It is accessible via a short dirt road that opens up onto a parking lot for cars, motorbikes and hotel tour buses (this spot is very popular). At this point, a trail a few metres long is all that separates you from the beach. Follow it and you'll find yourself at the edge of the sea on a beautiful fine-sand beach bounded by steep cliffs atop which stand some of Saint-Martin's luxurious residences. This is a wonderful place to soak up some rays. Unfortunately, slippery rocks lie along parts of the shore and swimmers must use caution to get beyond them. Also, the waves are often strong. A small drink stand and picnic tables have been set up for the public.

The beach at **Baie des Prunes ★** is another two kilometres farther along. Pay close attention, because a small sign indicating *"baignade non-surveillée"* (unsupervised swimming) is all that marks the trail leading to the beach. Bound by sea-grape trees growing haphazardly here and there, the beach seems deserted, lending it a certain charm. However, a short stroll along this long ribbon of soft, fine sand reveals beautiful residences hidden behind luxuriant vegetation. Slippery rocks are a nuisance here as well.

The sheer cliff known as **Falaise aux Oiseaux** marks the northern extremity of the beach. Lovely homes perched atop its summit overlook the azure waters. At the southern extremity of the beach is a path leading to Long Bay and passing through **Pointe du Canonnier**.

A third beach extends along the lowlands. As its name suggests, the beach at **Long Bay ★★** is the longest, but it is also the prettiest of the three. This beach could be divided into two distinct parts. The first, which lies farther west, has a wild appearance, much like the beach at Baie aux Prunes. Not very developed and bordered by rather wild vegetation, this beach is caressed by the ocean's inviting waves, which are not always easily accessible, as the beach and shoreline are also strewn with large rocks. The other part of the beach ends in sheer cliffs, which even the sea cannot succeed in conquering and at the summit of which stand the magnificent buildings of the La Samanna hotel (see p 98). The beach at the foot of these cliffs is more inviting to swimmers.

Around Pic Paradis

To reach the eastern part of the island, follow Rue de Hollande, which leads to the main road.

The road heads east and follows the coast for a while before leading inland. About two kilometres out of Marigot, you'll cross a dirt road weaving its way between Creole cottages to the seaside at **Friar's Bay** ★ (Baie des Pères). This isolated beach, bordered by palm trees, is washed by perpetually calm waters, making it a favourite with swimmers who prefer to avoid big waves. The beach also scores points with snorkellers, who come to explore the beautiful coral reefs offshore. Lined with a few beach restaurants, it attracts a young vacationing clientele with its beautiful beach and "cool" ambiance.

On the way back to the main road, you'll pass another road on your right barely a hundred metres after Friar's Bay. It is very narrow and climbs up a hill to Colombier.

Colombier

The tiny hamlet of **Colombier**, with its mere handful of humble abodes scattered here and there, remains unadulterated and far from the tourist villages. A stroll down its only street is like stepping into another world. Besides its Caribbean cachet, though, the village has little to offer. It is, however, of undeniable interest to travellers heading off on the **Sentier des Crêtes**. To reach this trail, take the road at the entrance to the village all the way to the end. You'll find a small pink house; the trail runs behind it, then continues on to St. Peters (Sint Maarten) and up Pic Paradis. If you hike the trail, make sure to bring enough water, as there is none available along the way or at the summit of Pic Paradis.

Many people choose to scale **Pic Paradis** (424 m), but if this hike seems too arduous you can always make the ascent by car. To do so, retrace your steps and follow the main road to Rambaud (one km). From there follow the town road as it meanders up to the summit. The road is steep and uneven, and seems almost impassable at times, but the **view** ★★ is stunning and well worth the effort. To get to the viewpoint, take the trail (which is in fact part of the "Route des Crêtes", see p 94) to the left of the France Télécom gates and follow it for some ten minutes. You will then reach a plateau where there are lookout points affording magnificent panoramas. Weather-permitting, you can even see some of the islets of the Caribbean chain in the distance.

By continuing on the main road towards Grand Case, you'll end up in Saint-Louis.

Saint-Louis

Stop off in **Saint-Louis**, a small cliff-top village with just a few houses, to take advantage of the spectacular **view ★** of the coast. There is no real lookout point, so you'll have to stop by the side of the road to take it all in.

Grand Case

Grand Case ★★ is without a doubt the most picturesque village on the island. There are no luxurious mansions, just a charming, typically Caribbean village whose beauty lies in its simplicity and its pretty colours. Extending along the shore, Grand Case consists of a series of small, vibrant Creole houses and emanates a wonderful holiday atmosphere. Residents live in harmony with the vast glittering expanse of sea, while visitors come to relax on the beautiful crescent of fine sand and contemplate the moored boats bobbing ever so gently in the calm waters. Don't forget the other reason people come to Grand Case: the excellent restaurants (see p 108)! All of these features make this a popular spot with vacationers.

Grand Case's charms are not all apparent to the naked eye, as some of them are more understated. Magical scenery lies concealed on the outskirts of the village. Offshore, the Caribbean Sea thrives with coral, multicoloured fish and a variety of plants – a veritable underwater paradise that visitors will have a chance to admire while diving. Several enterprises organize such excursions (see p 91).

SAINT-MARTIN

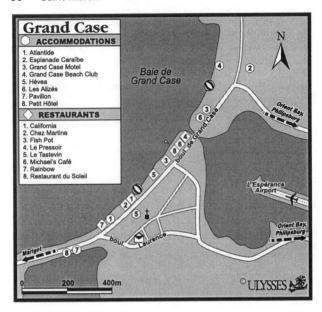

If the depths beckon but the thought of scuba gear doesn't, reserve a spot on the **Seaworld Explorer** ★ *(adults US$30/165 F, children US$18/100 F; departure from the pier at 11am, subject to change; ☎05.90.599-5-24-078)*, a semi-submersible boat with passenger seats in the hold; you are thus sitting more or less under the boat, and explore the sea-floor 15 metres below the surface. There are large portholes so that you can view the natural wonders. It's quite a trip!

Anse Marcel

From Grand Case, follow the main road east. First you will come to L'Espérance airport, then a few hundred metres farther you will cross a secondary road cutting off to the left. Follow it to the fork and stay left again to reach Anse Marcel.

Creole House

The road cuts through steep hills and reveals several beautiful **panoramas** ★. Then around a corner magnificent **Anse Marcel** ★ (*anse* means cove) appears. The town, nestled in verdant hills, extends along the sea and consists mainly of superb gardens and exquisite hotels (see p 100). A veritable haven of tranquillity, far from all traffic and noise, the setting is truly exceptional.

This spot is not easy to reach, however, since Anse Marcel is not served by public buses; visitors will therefore have to get there on their own. Furthermore, no doubt to discourage trespassers, guards are posted at the entrance, monitoring the comings and goings of visitors.

There is a pleasant **beach** ★ at Anse Marcel, but if isolated beaches are what you are looking for, follow the walking trail that starts at Anse Marcel and weaves its way through the foothills. It leads to the beautiful beach at **Baie des Petites Cayes**. This is the only way to reach this beach, except by boat.

The path continues, making its way to **Grandes Cayes** ★. Concealed behind the grass and shrub-covered hills, this beach, consisting of a few coves, is wild and not very busy; only seagrape trees clutter its blond sand. The turquoise ocean

SAINT-MARTIN

stretches out as far as the eye can see. Travellers can also get there by taking the dirt road that leaves from French Cul-de-Sac and runs alongside the hills to Grandes Cayes. If you decide to visit this beach, bring your beach umbrella, as there is no shade.

French Cul-de-Sac

If you want to go to French de Cul-de-Sac, coming from Grand Case by the main road, take the secondary road to your left (the one that also leads to Anse Marcel) all the way to the fork. This time take the fork to the right.

A small road leads to the northernmost tip of the island, a virtually uninhabited region that receives little rainfall. It does, however, boast a few lovely, quiet coves. Moreover, this, or more precisely the Étang de la Barrière, is the point from which the boats leave for Pinel Island.

The **Étang de la Barrière** is unique because of the stunning green tint of its waters. Unfortunately, there are a lot of seaweed and rocks, which may be unappealing to some visitors. There are a parking lot and a few stands on its banks selling various souvenirs such as T-shirts, sarongs and sculptures. Most people stop there on the way to Îlet Pinel.

The outline of **Îlet Pinel** ★ *(30 F return; 7am to 5pm)* is discernable off the shores of Baie de Cul-de-Sac. This tiny island is a great place to escape to, and enjoy the sandy beach and the sensation of being on a desert island far from the crowds. Water taxis shuttle passengers to Pinel Island, leaving (when full) from the Étang de la Barrière quay. You can also get there from Orient Bay, though this costs a little more.

The beach at Baie Orientale is also the place from which boat-taxis take visitors to **Île Tintamarre** *(US$10; every day, 7am to 5pm)*, located two kilometres off the coast. This island reserves some stunning underwater scenery for divers (see p 91).

Atlantic Coast

You can easily reach Orient Bay from the main road. Precise road signs show the way.

Orient Bay ★★★

If there's an image you'll cherish, it's bound to be of Orient Bay: a long ribbon of fine sand, stretching out as far as the eye can see, bordered by the shimmering waves of the Atlantic Ocean. This beach, unquestionably the loveliest on the island, is perpetually crowded with visitors who come here to enjoy water sports or the pleasures of a delightfully refreshing swim, or simply to have their skin caressed by the hot rays of the sun (prudent sun bathers will have brought their own parasol). Merchants have set up shop, offering all kinds of merchandise from souvenirs to sports equipment, beverages and food. Many will undoubtedly deplore this succession of unsightly stalls, which sticks out like a sore thumb in this otherwise magnificent tableau. Visitors will find consolation, however, in that this does little to mar the beach's unparalleled beauty. The beach welcomes nudists. The approaches to the bay have been protected by a new park; this entire area, where several hotels have been erected, is now a protected zone.

Baie de l'Embouchure

Travellers continuing along the road will reach the Baie de l'Embouchure; attentive drivers will notice the mangrove swamp that has developed here, but which was ravaged by Hurricane Luis. This strange forest, looking much like an impenetrable tangle, is composed of mangroves, trees whose long aerated roots enable them to grow in mud and water. Visitors will have to be content with observing it from afar, however, as there is no means of getting a closer look. The beach is hardly among the most beautiful on the island, but it is a favourable spot for windsurfers of all levels, as amateurs will find its banks well-sheltered from the winds, and more seasoned enthusiasts can take advantage of the strong winds blowing across the open sea.

SAINT-MARTIN

At the Baie de l'Embouchure you will notice a long structure that houses an unusual and captivating attraction: the **Butterfly Farm** ★ *(US$10; on Le Galion Beach, ☎05.90.87.31.21)*. Here you can discover the wondrous world of lepidopterans as you walk, accompanied by a guide, amongst an abundance of plants and several hundred freely fluttering butterflies representing some twenty species. Visitors will also be able to witness these insects' complete metamorphosis: caterpillars turning into cocoons, the development of pupa and the birth of multi-coloured butterflies. The tour lasts 20 to 25 minutes.

By following the road heading to Philipsburg, travellers will go through the village of **Orléans**.

Keep following the road until you arrive at the Baie Lucas.

Baie Lucas

Baie Lucas (Coralita Beach) is situated north of Oyster Pond. This bay is not as busy as the other two, no doubt because its banks are covered in seaweed. It remains, nonetheless, a pleasant beach of white sand.

Travellers continuing south will end up in Sint Maarten, the Dutch part of the island (see p 119).

 OUTDOOR ACTIVITIES

Ribbons of fine white sand extend between land and sea at various points along the island's periphery. These beaches are a veritable paradise for water sports enthusiasts. Hikers will find their own small paradise along the trails that crisscross the hills in the centre of the island. In fact, the island offers nature-lovers of all kinds a wide range of activities to choose from.

This section provides information on how to go about practising those activities, as well as addresses of places that rent out sports equipment.

Swimming

The island's beaches, each one lovelier than the last, have something to offer every kind of swimmer. There is only one nudist beach among them; it lies at the southern extremity of Orient Bay.

Descriptions of the best beaches can be found in the "Sights and Beaches" section of this chapter (see p 78).

Scuba Diving

Scuba diving enthusiasts will not be disappointed, for the island boasts a number of interesting sites. Coral reefs have developed off the coasts of Baie de Marigot, Friar's Bay, Baie aux Prunes and Grand Case bay. In Saint-Martin, the **Creole Rock** is one of the favoured diving sites for beginners, since a multitude of fish as well as magnificent corals can be seen here in waters no more than ten metres deep. Visitors can observe this wondrous world's fascinating underwater life by taking part in an excursion.

A few centres organize diving excursions:

Octopus: 15 Boulevard Grand Case, B.P. 072, Grand Case 97070, ☎05.90.87.20.62, ⬞05.90.87.20.63; dive: 230 F; resort course: 250 F; night dive: 260 F; excursion to Tintamarre: 290 F.

Blue Ocean: B.P. 940, Baie Nettlé 97060, ☎05.90.87.89.73. Dive: 250 F. Night dive: 330 F.

Sea Horse Diving: Mercure Simpson hotel beach, Baie Nettlé, ☎05.90.87.84.15

Sea Dolphin: Flamboyant hotel beach, Baie Nettlé, ☎05.90.87.60.72

Scuba Fun: Anse Marcel, ☎05.90.87.36.13. First dive: 450F.

SAINT-MARTIN

The deserted island of **Tintamarre** is especially renowned for its coral reefs; if this adventure sounds tempting, you can get there via several enterprises organizing excursions near this islet's coast, located two kilometres off the coast of Saint Martin. The excursion includes the crossing by boat, a diving survey of the coral depths and a picnic on one of the island's beautiful beaches.

Seasoned thrill-seeking divers might prefer an excursion off the coast of **Saba** (Dutch Antilles), whose dive sites (for experienced divers) hold the enviable title of the most beautiful in the Caribbean.

 Snorkelling

It doesn't take much to snorkel: a mask, a snorkel and some fins. Anyone can enjoy this activity, which is a good way to develop an appreciation for the richness of the underwater world. You can go snorkelling in the waters off most beaches, near the coral reefs inhabited by various underwater species. Most dive centres also organize snorkelling excursions.

Blue Ocean: Baie Nettlé; sea trip: 165 F.

At either end of **Orient Bay**, shopkeepers rent snorkelling equipment: 30 F for one hour or 55 F for the day.

Octopus: Grand Case; equipment rental: 45 F.

 Parasailing

Off the beaches of Orient Bay and Baie Nettlé, visitors will soon catch sight of parasailing buffs executing dizzying flights while suspended between earth and sky. This experience is not restricted to the intrepid elite, and you too can take part (if you don't suffer from vertigo). A few centres organize such adventures:

Blue Ocean: Baie Nettlé; one tour: 280 F.

Orient Bay: there is a stand at the edge of the beach; one tour: 280 F (US$50).

Sailing

Sailing is another enchanting way to explore the sea's crystal-line waves. Some centres organize excursions, while others rent out sailboats to experienced sailors.

Blue Ocean: Baie Nettlé; sailboat rental (Sunfish): 550 F per half-day.

Bikini Watersports: Orient Bay; catamaran rental: 500 F per half-day.

Windsurfing

Certain beaches on the island have won the favour of windsurfers, but only a few offer rollers and strong winds. In fact, the Baie de l'Embouchure beach may be the only one that is truly suited to this sport. Many, however, are ideal for beginners, and promise hours of fun. Baie de l'Embouchure, Friar's Bay, Orient Bay and Baie Nettlé are a few places where you can rent equipment and show off your skills.

Bikini Beach: Baie Orientale; rental: 100 F per hour.

Blue Ocean: Baie Nettlé; rental: 140 F.

Windy Reef: Baie de l'Embouchure; rental 100 F per hour, 400 F for 5 hours; courses also offered; ☎05.90.87.08.37.

Kayaking

Some centres, particularly on the beach in **Orient Bay**, rent out kayaks in which you can skim over the waves. Count on spending 60F an hour.

SAINT-MARTIN

Deep-sea Fishing

Anglers interested in the deep-sea experience can check out the following establishments:

Blue Ocean: Baie Nettlé; excursion: 2,500 F; ☎05.90.87.89.73.

Hôtel Méridien: Anse Marcel, ☎05.90.87.67.00.

 Jet-skiing

Jet-skis may be rented at:

Blue Ocean: Baie Nettlé; rental: 250 F per half hour.

Sally's Jet Watersports: Orient Bay; rental: 250 F per half hour.

 Hiking

As is the case with a number of Caribbean islands, the towns and villages of Saint Martin are scattered along its coasts, with very few hamlets in heart of the island itself. This area, rather, consists of a small mountainous massif whose highest summit reaches 424 metres: **Pic Paradis**. Though very few roads lead to this peak, it is crisscrossed by many small paths, as the inhabitants prefer cutting through the island to get from one end to the other rather than going around. These small paths, which actually only make up a single trail, called **"Route des Crêtes"**, link St. Peters to Mont Vernon, passing by Colombier and Pic Paradis. Totalling no less than 40 kilometres, Route des Crêtes literally winds its way around the massif, revealing fabulous panoramas in various spots along the way. Open to all, this trail is a good opportunity to discover Saint Martin's back country. Hikers should come prepared, however (see p 71) for the trail is long and offers very little shade (the island's vegetation is often limited and trees along the trail are few and far between), and neither water nor food are sold for most of the journey.

Although certain people see to the maintenance of the trails, nature often gets the upper hand here, especially after rain showers, when it can become a little harder to find the trail. You should therefore stay alert and be careful to remain on the trail so as not lose your way. Some parts of the trail are marked with paint on tree trunks.

Bicycling

For all intents and purposes, the island has one road, which cars speed along. It winds through the hills, and uphill sections are often steep. Furthermore, it is generally unshaded. There are also a few secondary roads, but you'll always have to take the main road to reach them. Bicycles are therefore not the ideal mode of transport on the island and few people use them. Bikes can nevertheless be rented at different places on the island. Expect to pay about 60 F per day.

Baie Nettlé: Location 2 Roues, ☎05.90.87.25.59

Horseback Riding

A few riding stables organize riding excursions, offering a pleasant way to discover the island.

OK-Coral: between the mouth of the Bay de l'Embouchure and Coralita Beach, ☎05.90.87.40.72.

Caïd and Isa: Anse Marcel, ☎05.90.87.45.70.

Bayside Riding Club: Baie de l'Embouchure, ☎05.90.87.36.64.

ACCOMMODATIONS

Marigot

Lodging is available in Marigot. There a few hotels, most of which offer an average level of comfort. Among them, the

Royal Louisiana *(440 F, bkfst incl.; Général de Gaulle, Marigot,* ☎/≠05.90.87.86.51) is worth mentioning. It is located right downtown and offers modest rooms.

If you want to stay in Marigot but also enjoy the pleasures of being close to the sea, the **Marina Royale** *(690 F; Rue St. James,* ☎05.90.87.52.46) hotel may be the perfect place. This tidy blue-and-white building has an enchanting site near the marina. Situated in the heart of the bustle, it offers decent rooms, some of which have a view of the marina.

A series of oceanfront buildings mark the entrance into Marigot. Among these is the blue-and-white **Hotel Beach Plaza** *(1238 F ocean view; ≈, ≡, ℜ, Baie de Marigot, 97150,* ☎05.90.87.87.00). Its delightful lobby, which pleasantly opens out onto the sea and boasts a magnificent view, leads to the rooms, some of which have a balcony overlooking the sea or the garden. These are, of course, the most prized, since the others have a less enviable view of the parking lot. However, all are comfortable.

Baie Nettlé

The western part of the island ends with a long, narrow strip of land that separates the Atlantic from the calm salty waters of Simson Bay Lagoon. This strip of land boasts several attractive beaches, and offers views out over the very different stretches of water on either side. Luxurious hotels have been built on both the Dutch and the French side.

Long stretches of fine-sand beaches are found all over the western point, some washed by the bay, others by the Atlantic. Baie Nettlé is the first beach west of Marigot. Luxurious hotel complexes have been built here and there.

Among the string of tourist complexes, the **Royal Beach** *(494 F; ≈, ≡, ℜ; B.P. 571, Baie Nettlé, 97056,* ☎05.90.87.89.89), situated behind the Baie Nettlé shopping centre, stands out for its lower prices. Built by the ocean, the hotel offers similar advantages to the other hotels in the area (a big pool, a beach, though it is a bit small, and a garden). Unfortunately, the building itself and the garden, which have both seen better days, are rather disappointing at first glance.

The **Laguna Beach** *(550 F; ≈, ≡, ℜ; Baie Nettlé, 97150, ☎05.90.87.91.75, ⊷05.90.87.81.65)* faces the Royal Beach and offers similarly-priced rooms of superior quality. The lobby is a large, somewhat inhospitable room. At one end is the restaurant, followed by the garden. The hotel boasts large, simply decorated rooms with pleasant balconies. It also comprises a lovely garden and a large swimming pool looking out on Simson Bay Lagoon.

The **Mercure Simson** *(1080 F bkfst incl.; ≈, K, ≡, ℜ, ⊛; B.P. 172, Baie Nettlé, 97150, ☎05.90.87.54.54, ⊷05.90.87.92.11)* hotel complex boasts a much more attractive location. The rooms, each with a large balcony and a view of the bay, are distributed among several buildings. The balcony is almost like an extra room, since it is both useful (the kitchenette is there) and pleasant. Mornings and late afternoons spent here are particularly delightful. The complex also has a large garden planted with brilliantly flowering bushes and, of course, a pool around which most of the day's activities take place.

The site of **Anse Margot** *(860 F; ≈, ≡, ℜ; 97150, ☎05.90.87.92.01, ⊷87.92.13)* provides vacationers with a relaxing and comfortable environment. The vast garden, which lies by the bay, is overgrown with plants, making it a pleasant place for a stroll. Here and there stand lovely light-pink-and-white stucco buildings, all of which have charming, elaborate balconies. The rooms inside are large, tastefully decorated and well kept.

The **Nettlé Bay** *(1,050 F for the villa, no bkfst incl., or 940 F for a room in the Gardens, bkfst incl.; ≈, ℜ, ≡, K; B.P. 4081, Baie Nettlé 97064, ☎05.90.87.68.68)* offers the same level of comfort as the Anse Margot, but features two types of accommodation: villas, which include one or two large rooms and a kitchenette, and the "Gardens", which is a series of bungalows, each with 35 rooms. All of the buildings have been designed to afford a view of the bay and the pool from each room.

SAINT-MARTIN

Amongst the posh, comfortable hotels on the bay, the **Flamboyant Resort** *(1200 F; ≈, ☺, ℛ, ≡, K; Baie Nettlé, 97150, ☎05.90.87.60.00)*, with its orange tile roofs, is worth mentioning. Besides its advantageous location on one of the best beaches on Baie Nettlé, it offers a whole range of services and facilities to ensure its guests an enjoyable stay, including two pools, hot-tubs, tennis courts and rooms with kitchenettes. It also has good-sized rooms of flawless comfort.

Long Bay

If a dream hotel exists, it could very well be **La Samanna** *(US$640 bkfst incl.; ≈, ℛ; B.P. 4077, Long Bay, ☎05.90.87.51.22, ≈05.90.87.87.86)*, built at the top of a cliff, near one the best beaches on the island, Long Bay. Its design takes full advantage of the unbeatable location. The restaurant, rooms and lobby face the sparkling waves, and no matter where you look the view is beautiful. Special attention has been taken with the decoration: for example, the lobby is adorned with a small ceramic-tile fountain, while the walls are covered with middle-Eastern tapestries, lending the area a particular charm. The comfortable rooms are also tastefully decorated.

Rambaud

Far from the hubbub of the city and the bustle of holiday villages, the **Garden Hill** *(500 F; ☺, K; ☎05.90.87.93.96, ≈05.90.87.26.02)* will particularly please those who appreciate quiet and remote places. Built at the very end of a steep road that winds down the side of a cliff, the beige building, adorned with lovely sky-blue friezes, dominates the region. Each of its charming rooms has a balcony from which you can take in this enchanting sight. The hotel is very pleasant, but keep in mind that you must have a car to get there as it is located in Rambaud, a hamlet situated between Marigot and Grand Case that boasts few services (no grocery store or restaurant, and a fair distance from the beach).

Grand Case

The pretty town of Grand Case has a good choice of accommodations sure to pelase, whether you're looking for medium-budget hotels or luxury complexes.

A few reasonably priced places, by Saint-Martin standards, are located in the centre of town. Among these, the **Hévea** *(420 F; 163 Boul. Grand Case, Grand Case, 95170, ☎05.90.87.56.85, ≈05.90.87.83.88)*, set up in a sweet little house, is worth a look. The rooms are far from luxurious, but are decorated with special attention, with wooden beams and antique furniture that lend them a singular charm. This small hotel has two rooms and six studios (three of which are air-conditioned). Good value for your money, but be forewarned that reservations are not always respected.

The **Grand Case Beach** *(450 F; K; Grand Case, 97150, ☎05.90.87.87.75, ≈05.90.87.26.55; or write to B.P. 175 Philipsburg, Sint Maarten)* motel also offers reasonably-priced rooms, which offer a basic level of comfort, and have the distinct advantage of including an equipped kitchenette. The decor is disappointing, but at least the rooms have a view of the sea.

Low-priced accommodation are available at **Les Alizés** *(450 F; 10 Allée des Escargots, 97150, ☎05.90.87.95.38, ≈05.90.29.31.71)* motel. There is nothing luxurious about the place; the rooms all offer rudimentary comfort (the bare minimum) and have a modest decor, but the establishment is located conveniently close to the beach.

🦐 The **Atlantide** *(600 F; K, ≈; B.P. 5140, Grand Case, 97150, ☎05.90.87.09.80, ≈05.90.87.12.36)* hotel was built just outside the centre of Grand Case, so guests are near the action, but still enjoy a quiet setting with direct access to the beach. Each prettily decorated, well-maintained room has a terrace looking out over the water so you can appreciate those beautiful seascapes. The reception is very friendly.

🦐 A lovely white residence, elegantly adorned with ceramic tiles, houses the **Petit Hôtel** *(US$250/1,500 F; ≈, K; 97150,*

☎*05.90.29.09.65, ↪05.90.87.09.19)*, a magnificent residence that is hardly luxurious, but quite comfortable. Guests stay in large, thoroughly comfortable rooms, charmingly decorated with woodwork. Though the establishment does not have the convenience of being right downtown (it is a short distance away), it has the advantage of being right by the ocean.

Right next door, the **Pavillon** *(950 F bkfst incl, studio; ≈, K; 97150,* ☎*05.90.87.96.46, ↪05.90.87.71.04)* also rents out rooms equipped with kitchenettes and beautiful terraces opening out on the waves. Its decor sports brighter, more tropical colours, and the rooms have pastel-coloured rattan furniture. The place is very well maintained.

You can't miss the buildings of the **Esplanade Caraïbe** *(1,500-1,800 F; ≈, ≈, K, ⊛; B.P. 5007, Grand Case, 97150,* ☎*05.90.87.06.55, ↪05.90.87.29.15)*, built on a hillside overlooking the bay of Grand Case. They are visible from town. Everything here ensures the comfort of the guests: the kitchenette is particularly well equipped, the studio sitting-rooms are spacious, the rooms are attractively decorated with beautiful woodwork (doorway, ceiling and staircase for the suites with mezzanine) and have sea views.

At the very end of Grand Case Beach stands the long, white one-storey building of the **Grand Case Beach Club** *(1,250 F; ≈, ≈, K; 97150,* ☎*05.90.87.51.87, ↪05.90.87.59.93)*. A tad old-fashioned, it comprises no less than 72 rooms, which are large and offer all modern conveniences as well as a balcony overlooking the beach. Moreover, a small, prettily laid-out garden borders the beach, where a host of water activities are organized. The establishment is a few minutes' walk from the village; guests can therefore easily enjoy the advantages of Grand Case while basking in peaceful surroundings.

Anse Marcel

No doubt attracted by the beauty of the location and the superb beach, several hotel complexes have been built around the little cove of Anse Marcel.

The **Hôtel Privilège** *(900-1,000 F; ≈; Anse Marcel, 97056, ☎05.90.87.37.37, ⊷05.90.87.33.75)* occupies a small section of Anse Marcel, back a bit from the beach. It is set up inside a quaint wooden building of typical Antillean charm. The ground floor of the building houses a row of shops. The airy rooms, located upstairs, are adorned with large windows looking out over the garden and are well furnished with pieces that don't overwhelm. Hammocks are strung up on the balconies.

Upon arriving in Anse Marcel, you'll notice a road climbing up into the hills. At the summit is the **Panoramic Privilege** *(1,884 F bkfst incl.; ≈, ℜ, ≡; Anse Marcel, 97150, ☎05.90.87.38.38, ⊷05.90.87.44.12)*hotel complex. It may not be right on the beach, but it does offer an exceptional view of Anse Marcel and a tranquil setting ideal for people looking for relaxation. The rooms have balconies from which to contemplate the sea, and tennis courts and a spa are available for the use of guests. The complex also comprises the **Horizon** hotel, which has attractive, cheerfully-coloured rooms, all equipped with large bathrooms.

The **Caye Blanche** *(1,900 F; ≈, ≡, K; 97150, ☎05.90.87.30.30, ⊷05.90.87.48.55)* has opted for a decor that is unique in Saint-Martin: it manages to imbue the rooms with a soothing quality and keeps guests cool no matter what time of day. This is achieved with a pinkish-tiled floor, white walls and sofas and a few pieces of wooden furniture. The bathrooms feature pretty coloured tiles, which are a pleasant addition and complement the simple, refined decor of this establishment, one of the loveliest in Saint-Martin. The entire hotel is of flawless elegance; the terraces, appointed with teak furniture, look out on the pool and quiet garden. Some rooms are equipped with kitchenettes, and a cook is available upon request.

Le **Méridien** *(ℜ, ≡, ≈; B.P. 581, Anse Marcel, 97056, ☎05.90.87.67.00, ⊷05.90.87.30.38)*, a vast hotel complex containing **L'Habitation Lonvilliers** *(1,670 F)* and **Le Domaine** *(1,850 F)*, occupies almost all of Anse Marcel. A vast garden with a profusion of flowering plants, ideal for a stroll, surrounds these buildings, and the whole setup is surrounded by the beach and the sea. L'Habitation de Lonvilliers has very beautiful rooms. Recently built right next door, Le Domaine offers equally

SAINT-MARTIN

comfortable rooms. A bamboo-lined lane leads the way. It goes without saying that the setting is superb and very peaceful.

Cul-de-Sac

Compared to the other beaches on the island, the Baie de Cul-de-Sac is under-developed. There are, however, a few hotels, including the **Belvedere Residence** *(2,400 F per week; Cul-de-Sac, 97150, ☎05.90.87.37.89, ⊶05.90.87.30.52)*, on a hillside in an unfortunately dull setting. The rooms are comfortable but only somewhat make up for this drawback. Guests have the use of a big pool.

Mont Vernon

The **Jardins de Chevrisse** *(570 F studio, 790 F villa; ≈, K; 97150, ☎05.90.87.37.79, ⊶05.90.87.38.03)* comprises several yellow-walled, orange-roofed cottages, built in close proximity to each other. These close quarters are certainly not conducive to intimacy, but the rooms are quite acceptable. A profusion of plants makes the rooms and their terraces somewhat more private.

The **Mont Vernon** *(1,290 F, 2,290 F with sea view; ≈, ≈, ℜ; B.P. 1174, 97062, ☎05.90.87.62.00, ⊶05.90.87.37.27)* hotel stands at the foot of the hill of the same name, which lies at the northern tip of Orient Bay. Standing five storeys tall, the buildings, fitted out with blue, green or pink balconies, house large rooms, decorated with rattan furniture of the same colours. Guests also benefit from a vast and pleasant garden, which extends to Orient Bay's magnificent beach.

The **Alizea** *(1,080 F bkfst. incl.; ≈, ℜ, ≈, K; 25 Mont Vernon, Orient Bay, ☎05.90.87.33.42, ⊶05.90.87.41.15)* hotel is a bit far from the beach, but offers a spectacular view from its location above the shimmering waves. Guests enjoy comfortable studios with equipped kitchenettes in a pleasant setting.

Orient Bay

Skirting the ribbon of fine sand that trims the superb Orient Bay is a row of hotel complexes built to cater to guests seeking out one of the prettiest spots on the island.

🏨 **La Plantation** *(860 F studio bkfst incl., 1,180 F suite bkfst incl.; K, ≈, ≡; Orient Bay, 97150, ☎05.90.97.32.04, ⊷05.90.87.35.76)* hotel offers reasonably-priced accommodation in a magnificent setting that is unfortunately not right on the beach. The rooms are in quaint but modestly-decorated villas, and are quite comfortable. For the price, this is a good address to remember.

With a mere 28 rooms, **Hoste** *(1,110 F garden view, 1,200 sea view; ≈ ≡; 97150, ☎05.90.87.42.08, ⊷05.90.87.39.96)* combines the intimacy of a small hotel with the comfort of larger establishments. Its charming pastel-coloured bungalows have a lovely view of the bay and house simply-decorated but comfortable rooms. Moreover, guests will be treated to friendly and attentive service.

The **St. Tropez** *(935 F 1st floor, 1,045 F view of sea or garden; ≈, ≡; Orient Bay, ☎05.90.87.42.01, ⊷05.90.87.41.69)*, located on a small plot of land, attempts to use every square metre to its advantage, grouping together the Boca Raton, Capri and Palm Beach hotels. Several buildings of different styles have been constructed, housing 84 pleasantly-decorated suites. Though we could fault the tiny garden, the place is well located, with access to the beach.

🏨 The superb **Esmerelda** *(1,500 F, 2,200 F sea view; ≈, ≡, ℛ; 97071, ☎05.90.87.36.36, ⊷05.90.61.05.44)* complex consists of several luxurious villas in a vast garden graced with an abundance of plants and flowers. Each of the bungalows, at a fair distance from each other, have only a few rooms and each offers guests the luxury of a virtually private pool. The rooms, charmingly adorned with rattan furniture, warm colours and flowers, are another good reason to opt for this establishment.

The profusion of flowering oleanders and red hibiscus is a pleasant surprise upon entering the **Orient Bay Hotel** *(570 F studio, 790 villa; ≈, ≡, K; Mont Vernon 1, Route Cul-de-Sac, Orient Bay, 97150, ☎05.90.97.31.10, ⬐05.90.87.37.66)* and makes up for the lack of a garden. The blaze of colour also brightens up the pale pink villas. These are located in an area set back from the beach, but a nice pool makes up for this.

Located close by is the luxurious **Green Cay Village** *(13,972 F per week; ≈, ≡, ℜ, K; B.P. 3006, Orient Bay, 97064, ☎05.90.87.38.63, ⬐05.90.87.39.27)*. The goal here is to satisfy guests looking for peace and quiet. Accordingly, the rooms are not crammed into large buildings, but rather guests stay in charming, beautifully-decorated little houses, each with a private pool and a lovely terrace offering a view of the sea.

Club Orient *(1,230 F; ℜ, K; Orient Bay, 97150, ☎05.90.87.33.85, ⬐05.90.87.33.76)* is Saint-Martin's one and only clothing-optional resort. It consists of a series of wooden-slat cottages, scattered over extensive seaside grounds, brightened up here and there by a palm tree or a few bushes. Guests here enjoy unfettered comfort; indeed, this peaceful and secluded site is a true little paradise. However, the beach and the facilities are not reserved exclusively for naturists, and are open to all.

 RESTAURANTS

Marigot

Wonderful meals complemented by a view of either the Baie de Marigot or the marina can be enjoyed at several spots around town.

Sandwiches and pastries are easy to find for lunch or breakfast. **Delices de France** *($)*, on Rue Général de Gaulle, sells delicious croissants and *pains au chocolat* (chocolate croissants) early in the morning. The lunchtime menu (around 50 F) is very simple, made up essentially of quiches and sandwiches.

If you happen to walk along Rue de la Liberté, next to the courthouse you'll see a **Boulangerie-Pâtisserie** *($)* which also serves sandwiches and salads. It has an attractive terrace that is popular at noon, even though it's right on the street.

The **Bar de la Mer** *($$-$$$; 1 Rue de la Liberté, ☎05.90.87.81.79)* is a good place to enjoy a waterfront terrace. The tasty food and relaxed atmosphere are what attract diners here. Most come at lunchtime for the salads and fish dishes. Barbecue days are particularly popular: the cook presides over the grill, broiling steak, fish and seafood, the aromas of which fill the air.

The marina also attracts crowds of people. It is a pleasant spot with many restaurants offering simple menus (grilled fish, salad). They are located one next to the other, and each has a cozy terrace with a view of the marina. Among these, **Belle Époque** *($$-$$$; ☎05.90.87.70.70)* serves meals of good value that includes a starter, dessert and an utterly delicious grilled rock lobster.

Next door, the **Chanteclair** *($$$; ☎05.90.87.94.60)*, also on the marina, is another enjoyable place. The choice of dishes, each more succulent than the last, is extensive. A few tasty examples are the *thon grillé avec légumes au vinaigre balsamique* (grilled tuna with vegetables in balsamic vinegar) or the *Saint-Jacques bardées de magret*. If you're in the mood for Creole specialties, you can opt for the Caribbean menu, which offers such treats as *vivaneau grillé* (grilled red snapper) and coconut pie.

Still at the marina, though slightly removed from the bustle, the **Bistrot des Arts** *($$$; ☎05.90.87.55.20)* is a tad more chic. Day after day, delectable and attractively presented fish dishes such as the fillet of red snapper with Cajun sauce or grilled tuna steak with Creole sauce are prepared, as well as delicious meat dishes. The dessert menu's selections are equally tempting, and round out the meal beautifully.

Located at the very centre of town, outside the major tourist areas that are the marina and the bay, **La Chamade** *($$$; Rue St. James, ☎05.90.27.07.18)* easily passes unnoticed. And yet it is well worth the trip, particularly for those

SAINT-MARTIN

more concerned with the contents of their plates than an ocean view. The dining room is charming, with its brick wall and wooden furnishings. But the menu, prepared daily with care so as to offer diners quality ingredients and always-savoury dishes, is what truly makes this place outstanding. Some of the dishes are among the classics of French cuisine, notably the *confit de canard* (conserve of duck) and the *magret de canard au foie gras* (breast of duck with foie gras), while others are more innovative, like the grilled lobster Provençale with Pernod sauce. The starters are just as delicious, especially the escargots nestled in a puff pastry with morel sauce. Irrefutably one of the city's crowning jewels.

The **Mini-Club** *($$$; Rue de la Liberté, ☎05.90.87.50.69)* is Marigot's oldest restaurant and, year after year, its cuisine never disappoints. Whether you're in the mood for fish, stuffed crab or some kind of Creole specialty, this is the place to go in the city. Moreover, the place has a pleasant location right on the bay.

In the centre of town, away from the sea, is the **Charolais** *($$$$; Rue Félix Éboué, ☎05.90.87.93.19)*. The beach feels far away here, since the decor is more along the lines of an American ranch, with wooden walls decorated with troughs, pitchforks and cattle-breeding tools. This decor was chosen in accordance with the house specialty: beef, always top quality and always served in generous portions.

🦞 Housed in a magnificent colonial home, **La Vie en Rose** *($$$$; Boulevard de France, ☎05.90.87.54.42)* unquestionably ranks among the city's best restaurants. The dining room, very lovely and fitted out with a magnificent coffered ceiling, is very inviting. It is in this unparalleled environment that you will savour your meal... and what a meal! Choosing among the selection of dishes is already a delightful dilemma. A few are worthy of mention, most notably the *roulé de sole aux médaillons de langouste* a veritable feast for the palate. Diners can also choose to eat on the terrace, with its beautiful wrought-iron balcony. A host of small details, such as greeting guests with delicious appetizers, help make the evening a great success. At lunchtime, visitors can also dine on the other terrace, which looks out on the market. Service is very attentive.

Friar's Bay (Baie des Pères)

The beachfront **Friar's Bay Beach Café** *($-$$)*, where you can enjoy your meal right on the sand, is hard to miss. Served here are good and simple dishes, such as smoked chicken, salads and burgers, perfect for lunch if you do not wish to stray from the beach.

Sandy Ground

The lovely roadside Creole house that harbours the **Casa Créole** *($$-$$$;* ☎*05.90.87.28.45)* is a good place to keep in mind when you're in the mood for typical Creole fare, notably such treats as *blaff*, curries and court-bouillon.

The **Marios Bistrot** *($$$-$$$$)* stands on the edge of the arm of the sea that links the Caribbean Sea to Simson Bay Lagoon, and its dining room pleasantly overhangs the water. The restaurant also has a lovely decor, composed of sky-blue walls, ceramic tiles and beautiful lamps. An inviting ambiance radiates from this room, perfect for romantic dinners. The menu will also satisfy guests, for it offers refined dishes such as *poêlée de Saint-Jacques au risotto à la crème de crabe* or *panequet de saumon*, always succulently-prepared. Guests must also make a point of saving room for dessert, as the menu offers so many sublime goodies.

Baie Nettlé

For a change from buffets, you can have breakfast at **Chez Swan** *($)*, located in the Baie Nettlé shopping centre.

If you prefer a change of pace, head to **Bac Lien** *($$$;* ☎*05.90.87.90.23)* which serves Vietnamese and Thai special-ties. There isn't anything spectacular about these dishes, but they make for a nice change from Creole and French.

SAINT-MARTIN

Long Bay

You are sure to spend an unforgettable evening – one that will please your stomach as well as your wallet – at the La Samanna hotel's (see p 98) **Restaurant** *($$$$)*, where you will benefit from a magnificent dining room, offering an unobstructed view of the ocean and an elegant yet relaxed atmosphere. The menu varies according to what is available, but the dishes, artfully concocted and made from the freshest products on the market, are always a real treat.

Grand Case

Charming little Grand Case has a surprising number of good restaurants along its main street. Each menu is more appetizing than the last, making it difficult to choose where to eat.

Right on the edge of the beach, **Michael's Café** *($-$$)* is another friendly place in Grand Case for breakfast or lunch. Sandwiches and hamburgers are chief among the noontime offerings.

For a delicious pizza along the ocean, head to **California** *($$)*. If you prefer to eat in your room, keep in mind that this restaurant prepares food to go.

If you like authenticity, you simply have to eat a grilled fish from one of the **waterfront stands** *($-$$)*. Saint-Martin locals arrive at their weather-beaten wooden shacks in the early morning to begin preparing dishes of grilled fish and crab on make-shift barbecues. Despite these meagre facilities they concoct some divine little morsels.

To enjoy a good lunch without having to break the bank, head to the **Restaurant du Soleil** *($$-$$$; ☎05.90.87.92.32)*, which offers a decent bite to eat. Patrons here can sample a Niçoise salad or an exotic salad (large prawns and pineapple), quiche Lorraine or an omelette while comfortably seated in a lovely blue-and-yellow dining room, beyond which the sea stretches out into the distance.

One of Grand Case's fine restaurants, the **Rainbow** *($$$-$$$$)* has the advantage of being located right by the ocean. Guests will savour fish and seafood dishes in a lovely dining room with a simple and sparse decor, essentially adorned with flowering plants. Among the specialties, you can try the mahi-mahi in Creole sauce or the *poêlée de gambas* (pan-fried prawns), exquisitely served. The atmosphere is peaceful and service is courteous.

Come evening, some will undoubtedly wish to partake of an excellent meal in a quietly refined ambiance. Considered one of the best restaurants in town, **Chez Martine** *($$$-$$$$; ☎05.90.87.51.59)* will enchant the most discerning of gourmets with the exceptional quality of its dishes. The menu offers skilfully prepared dishes, such as the *médaillon de langouste à l'américaine*. Though servings are quite generous, keeping aside a little room for dessert is an absolute must, notably for the *gratin de fruits* or the passion fruit sorbet, a perfect blend of sweetness and tartness. Small extra touches as well as warm and attentive service help make the evening a great success.

Just a few steps beyond you'll come upon another restaurant with an equally delightful menu, **Le Tastevin** *($$$$; ☎05.90.87.55.47)*. All of the dishes are delicious, including the *daurade de saumon aux agrumes* (salmon with citrus fruits). The 340 F set menu is another possibility, offering an enticing choice of dishes, each accompanied by a glass of astutely chosen wine.

The **Fish Pot** *($$$$; ☎05.90.87.50.88)* has a long-established reputation and is always spoken of with a sigh of satisfaction. The reason for this is quite simple: it is one of those places where the lobster, red snapper, shrimp and other bounties from the sea are always fresh and divinely prepared. Such an establishment has earned a certain standing and, without being stuffy, ranks among the city's most elegant restaurants.

A fully renovated Creole house harbours one of the best restaurants in town, **Le Pressoir** *($$$$; ☎05.90.87.76.62)*, whose menu heralds the feast awaiting you within. Whether you opt for the green house salad or the fish soup with rouille, your meal will start off with a flourish. The equally delicious main courses include such delectable dishes as navarin lobster

SAINT-MARTIN

with herb sauce and salmon with puréed asparagus. Finally, the menu would hardly be complete without offering a decadent treat for dessert, including *gratin de fruits rouges*, made with red berries and currants, and a chocolate dessert with pear sauce. The service is courteous and you are sure to pass a pleasant evening here.

Anse Marcel

🦞 Just before the road leading to Anse Marcel there is a modest-looking establishment by the name of **Cotonier** *($$$; ☎05.90.87.44.56)* which serves some of the best Creole dishes on the island. People come from far and wide to taste these always innovative specialties, which include *filet de vivaneau au soufflé de mousse de lambi et beurre d'estragon* (filet of red snapper with shellfish mousse and tarragon butter) or the *roulade de volaille au boudin créole*. Your mouth will water just reading the menu, and the meal won't disappoint.

In Anse Marcel, visitors can choose between the restaurants in the Hotel Méridien: the **Barbecue** *($$$)* buffet located by the water and serving Caribbean specialties, or the **Belle France** *($$$$)*, which specializes in more refined French cuisine.

There is another restaurant outside the hotel complex, **La Louisiane**. The name is misleading, since the place does not serve Cajun food. Instead, visitors will find some well-prepared fish and meat dishes as well as salads and pizzas. Besides good food, the restaurant features a pleasant, simple decor and a friendly ambience. The place is just as enticing at lunchtime *($$)*, when the menu features reasonably priced daily specials, as in the evening *($$$)*, when you can choose among a good selection of dishes.

Mont Vernon

The **Taitu** *($$)* is a good spot to keep in mind for lunch, when you can enjoy an omelette, a sandwich or some Creole specialty while comfortably seated on the terrace surrounded by lush greenery.

The restaurant of the hotel **Mont Vernon** *($$-$$$)* has two dining rooms, one in an interior courtyard where each table boasts a lovely blue beach umbrella, and the other inside, attractively adorned with rattan furniture. In a convivial atmosphere, guests can savour various dishes ranging from Creole *accras* to hamburgers, not to mention a wonderful selection of fish and meat dishes.

Orient Bay

You won't find any fancy restaurants on the shores of Orient Bay, but there is a good selection of seaside restaurants serving simple and varied fare from pizza to hamburgers, not to mention sandwiches, salads and Mexican food. People tend to stop by between swims, and a friendly and relaxed atmosphere prevails. Among these restaurants, the **Bikini Beach** *($$-$$$)* stands out because of its large dining room, opening out on the beach, and its festive atmosphere. The menu offers meals that are hardly extravagant and a little pricey, but which make good lunch fare.

 ENTERTAINMENT

The sun sets early over Saint Martin, around 7pm; and it gets very dark. This doesn't mean the island has no nightlife, though – quite the contrary, in fact! Discotheques, bars and casinos start welcoming revellers in the late afternoon, when seaside spots offer drinks complemented by the spectacle of the setting sun. The excitement reaches its pinnacle during Carnival time.

Bars and Nightclubs

Baie Nettlé, Long Bay and Anse Marcel

Several popular locales near the tourist villages are known for their lively atmosphere or as great spots to pass the night away.

SAINT-MARTIN

The large hotel complexes, be it the Méridien (Anse Marcel), the Flamboyant (Baie Nettlé), the Mercure Simson (Baie Nettlé) or La Samanna (Long Bay), all have lovely bars offering magnificent ocean views.

On the hills overlooking Anse Marcel is the **Privilège Resort** hotel, which, aside from a magnificent view, has a lively piano bar.

Marigot

The **Bar de la Mer** *(port of Marigot)* has a pretty terrace with a view of the sea. People come to enjoy the relaxed atmosphere and chat with friends.

To end the night on a lively note and dance to your heart's content, you can check out one of two dance clubs that have made a name for themselves; **Club One** *(Marina la Royale, ☎05.90.87.98.41)* and **Privé** *(at the city's west entrance, Rue de la Liberté, ☎05.90.87.95.77)*, which has a great terrace.

Friar's Bay (Baie des Pères)

Musicians are often invited to play on the banks of Friar's Bay on Sundays, creating a festive ambiance that reigns throughout the afternoon.

Orient Bay

Several restaurants opening out on Orient Bay are great spots to while away your vacation with a late afternoon drink. On certain days, musicians come and play by the seaside.

Casinos

Though there are casinos only on the Dutch side of the island, no less than eight occupy the small territory of Sint Maarten (see p 138). Many of the hotels on the French side have free shuttle services for high-rolling guests looking for a little lady luck.

 SHOPPING

The boutiques are numerous, the products countless; we have selected a few of the more interesting places, either because of the products they sell, or the prices.

Marigot

Clothing

Marigot is truly the centre of high fashion in Saint-Martin. By poking around a little, and if you're not averse to spending money, you'll be able to find a few of the great French and Italian designers' latest creations.

Les Gens de... *(Rue du Général de Gaulle)*, **Milano** *(Rue du Général de Gaulle)* and **Romana** *(Rue de la République)* are among the beautiful boutiques where you can allow yourself to succumb to temptation.

Other shopkeepers have opted for clothing lines that are more suitable for the Caribbean climate, of a simpler style, often made of cotton or linen. Several lovely boutique have set up shop around the marina; you will thus be spoiled for choice among dresses, sarongs, skirts and tops, well suited to the tropical climate.

For great, bright-coloured T-shirts, head to **Comptoir des Îles** *(Rue de la Liberté)*.

Parents seeking clothes for their children will find just what they're looking for at **Pomme** *(Rue de l'Anguille)*.

SAINT-MARTIN

Looking for a swimsuit in the latest style? Drop by **Canicule Beach Wear** *(Rue du Président Kennedy)*, which carries a fine assortment of designs.

The **market** is held Wednesday and Saturday mornings, but several merchants set up shop here every day during tourist season to sell all types of clothes: swimsuits, sarongs, T-shirts, shorts, cotton pants, dresses — in short, everything to suit all tastes. Wonderful seashell, silver and coral jewellery, as well as curios and souvenirs of all kinds can also be found here.

Accessories

What can we say that hasn't already been said about **Lancel** *(Rue du Général de Gaulle)*, as well known for its leather bags as for its magnificent selection of accessories.

Belts, handbags, fun jewellery: there you have an idea of the small treasures that appeal to everyone and can be found at the boutique **Vie Privée** *(near the marina)*.

Jewellery

Several boutiques in Saint-Martin sell an abundance of fabulous Cartier jewellery, Lalique or Daum crystal vases and high quality leather goods. Even if you don't plan on buying anything, a visit to one of these places is a real feast for the eyes. **Goldfinger** *(Port la Royale marina)*, **Carat** *(Rue de la République)*, **Cartier** *(Rue de la République)*, **La Romana** *(Rue de la République)* and **Little Switzerland** *(Rue de la République)* are among the best of them.

Other boutiques, like **Passions** *(Rue du Général de Gaulle)*, offer more affordable jewellery made of mother-of-pearl, seashells or silver.

You will find very cute, reasonably priced coral necklaces and bracelets at **Schéhérazade** *(Rue du Général de Gaulle)*. Some of the gold jewellery is more expensive.

Perfume and Cosmetics

Prices of beauty products and perfume are on par with those in North America and Europe. There are therefore no real bargains to be had here.

Lipstick *(Rue du Président Kennedy and Rue de la République)*

Beauty and Scents *(Rue du Général de Gaulle)*

Wine and Spirits

For a stunning collection of vintage wines as well as more affordable bottles, you must check out **Goût du Vin** *(Rue de l'Anguille)*, where you are sure to find something to satisfy your palate.

Souvenirs and Gifts

For more information on one of Saint-Martin's more renowned artists, make a stop at **Galerie de Roland Richardson** *(Rue de la République)*, where a few of this painter's works are exhibited and sold. The paintings of A. Minguet, exhibited at **Chez Minguet** *(Rue de la Liberté)*, also make lovely gifts. Antique furniture and *objets d'art* so lovely that few can resist: visitors will likely give in to such temptations at **Mahogany**.

Creole arts and crafts, china and lace are among the little gifts to be found at the **Paris Art et Cadeaux** *(Rue du Président Kennedy)*, **Primavera** *(Rue du Général de Gaulle)* and **Papagayo** *(Rue du Général de Gaulle)* boutiques.

Groceries

For groceries, be it sausages, frozen foods, cookies or any other food product, head to the **Match** supermarket *(on the road leading to Grand Case)*.

Baie Nettlé

A small shopping centre has sprouted near Baie Nettlé's hotel complexes. In addition to two little restaurants serving breakfast, the mall comprises a well-stocked **grocery store** (wine, pastries, frozen food, cookies, chips) as well as a small shop where you can pick up **books, newspapers and magazines**.

Grand Case

Clothing

PEER sells lovely beach gear, notably clothing, bags, towels and swimsuits.

Newspapers and Magazines

On Boulevard Grand Case, next to the Fish Pot, you can stock up on magazines and newspapers at **Paragraphe**.

Souvenirs and Gifts

Graffiti *(Boulevard de Grand Case)* is a little shop where painted statuettes, fun t-shirts, curios and a thousand and one Caribbean souvenirs are piled up higgledy-piggledy.

The delightful boutique **Sexy Fruits** *(Boulevard de Grand Case)* is the place to go if you're shopping for a straw hat, a T-shirt, silver jewellery or a *paréo*.

Groceries

Tony's *(Boulevard Grand Case, opposite the California restaurant)* grocery store is no supermarket, but can come in handy in a pinch for such essentials as water, cookies and other foodstuffs.

Anse Marcel

Clothing

At **Art Caraib**, there are no extravagant garments, but rather a lovely collection of silk *paréos*, scarves and a whole assortment of cotton dresses.

Souvenirs and Gifts

For red or blue coral jewellery, mother-of-pearl statuettes, or any other little treat, you must make a stop at **Schéhérazade**.

Sporting Gear

Fans of water sports are sure to appreciate **Budget Marine**, which sells all manner of accessories, from fishing and scuba-diving gear to compasses and life jackets.

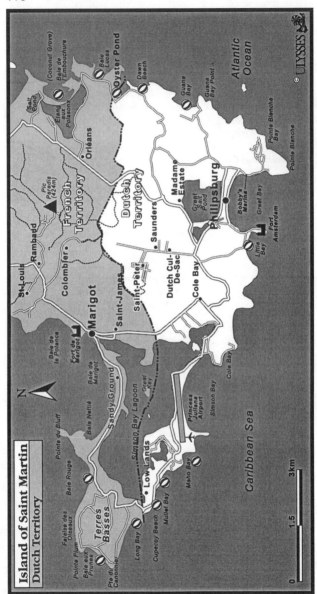

DUTCH SINTMAARTEN

S alt is at the root of the history of Sint Maarten. The Arawaks had already named the island of Saint Martin *sualouiga*, with means "land of salt", when this white substance first drew the attention of Dutch conquerors who settled in 1531 with the intention of exploiting this resource. This labour-intensive industry was the source of the prosperity of the Dutch, who were the only ones to extract salt from Great Salt Pond until the 20th century. Philipsburg developed beside this salt-marsh and today luxurious shops assure work for many people in this great commercial city. The 1970s saw tourist towns like Mullet Bay and Oyster Pond come into their own. Thanks to magnificent beaches, they still enchant crowds of visitors who return year after year.

 FINDING YOUR WAY AROUND

By Car

The 33 square kilometres of the Dutch part of the island are transected by very few roads. Most of these are in relatively good condition, although potholes here and there are an inconvenience. The most troublesome aspect of driving is the frequent deficiency, and occasional absence, of road signs, which makes it necessary to be very attentive.

From the Princess Juliana airport there is only one road heading west. It passes the tourist village of Mullet Bay, leads to Cupecoy, and then enters the French portion of the island at Terres Basses.

To reach Philipsburg (10 km from the airport), take the same road eastward. The road forks just before the city; the right lane heads downtown, and the left circles Great Salt Pond and heads into the interior, toward the hamlets of Madame Estate and Saunders.

To reach Dawn Beach and Oyster Pond, follow the main road (the one toward Madame Estate) and take the respective turn-offs for these destinations.

Renting a Car

Princess Juliana Airport

Avis: ☎52-316
Budget: ☎54-030
Europcar: ☎42-168
Hertz: ☎54-541
Safari: ☎53-186
Sandyg: ☎53-335

By Taxi

Reaching Mullet Bay and Philipsburg from the airport by taxi is simple, as there are plenty of cabs at the airport.

Airport: the taxi stand is in front of the exit.

Philipsburg: the taxi stand is on Frontstreet, next to the pier.

By Bus

Buses travelling the main road are relatively frequent, and during the day it is not difficult to reach the airport, Mullet Bay, Philipsburg, Marigot or Orient Bay. It can be more difficult to reach smaller, isolated beaches.

Philipsburg: bus stops are on Backstreet.

 PRACTICAL INFORMATION

Tourist Information

St. Maarten Tourist Bureau: 23 Walter Nisbeth Road, Philipsburg, ☎22-337, ⚏22-734

Banks

Bank of Nova Scotia: Backstreet, Philipsburg, ☎24-262.

Barclay's Bank: Frontstreet, Philipsburg, ☎22-567.

Chase Manhattan Bank: Philipsburg, ☎22-801.

Post Office

Philipsburg: at the corner of Vlaun and Richardson streets, ☎22-289; Mon to Thu 7:30am to 5pm, Fri 7:30am to 4:30pm.

Medical Care

Cay Hill Hospital: ☎31-111

Pharmacy: Philipsburg, ☎22-321

Emergency: ☎22-112

Ambulance: ☎22-111

Central Drugstore: Philipsburg, ☎22-321

  SIGHTS AND BEACHES

In the Dutch part of the island, there is but one large city, Philipsburg, the heart of economic activity around which many residential neighbourhoods have grown. Philipsburg certainly is worth visiting, but it is not really the reason people travel to Sint Maarten. They are more attracted to the tourist enclaves, such as Oyster Pond and Mullet Bay, that have been built at the edges of superb beaches of golden sand.

Philipsburg

Philipsburg ★ was built on a thin strip of land bordered by Great Bay on one side and a vast saltern on the other. It was founded in 1763 by Commander John Philips. Much before this date, however, in 1631, the Dutch had established themselves here, wanting to make use of this advantageous site (and of the immense salt deposits of Great Salt Pond). To protect the first colonists, **Fort Amsterdam ★** was erected at the eastern tip of the bay, at Little Bay.

This fort did not resist attack long; Spanish soldiers conquered it only two years later, and a large garrison charged with protecting the Spanish fleet set up camp. Bit by bit, this strategic choice proved less judicious, and in 1648 the Spanish abandoned Saint Martin, leaving a destroyed fort in their wake. That same year, the Dutch claimed a part of the island. The fort was rebuilt shortly thereafter and protected the territory until the 19th century. The ruins of Fort Amsterdam are now open to the public and if you visit them you will also be treated to a magnificent view of the city.

From morning to night, bustling Philipsburg is overrun by fervent crowds of visitors disembarking from cruise-ships anchored in the bay or arriving from the nearby tourist villages. They all come to shop in the city's boutiques which offer an incredible variety of goods. Clustered mostly along Frontstreet,

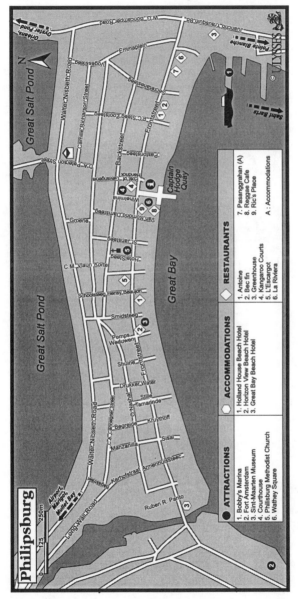

Philipsburg Methodist Church

the boutiques are lined up one after the other, with no shortage of sales and each more of a deal than the last, to keep the shoppers coming. For some, the powerful noon-day sun makes Philipsburg unbearable, while others thrive on the hustle and bustle.

Among this abundance of shop windows overflowing with gold jewellery, beauty products and liquor bottles are some lovely, pastel-coloured cottages. Strolling along the street, **Philipsburg Methodist Church** with a shingled facade stands prettily between Hotelsteeg and St. Jansteeg streets.

A few steps away, facing the pier and Wathey Square, is a beautiful white building which houses the **Courthouse ★**. In 1792, the commander of Sint Maarten, Mr. Willem Hendrik

Courthouse

Rink, ordered the construction of this building, since until then he had been governing from his own home, located at Cul-de-Sac, a great distance from Philipsburg. The architect John Handleigh was chosen to design it, and the next year, in 1793, the Courthouse was inaugurated. The stone walls enclose various rooms, including an office for the secretary of the governor as well as a few prison cells. The building was damaged by a hurricane in 1819 and it was not repaired until 1826, when a few modifications were made including the addition of a small bell tower. Over the years this building has served successively as a fire station, a prison, and finally a post office, and today it is very much a symbol of the island.

Finally, if you are interested in learning more about the Arawaks, the original inhabitants of the island, head to the **Sint Maarten Museum** *(US$2; closed Sun)* located in a simple house is right in the heart of the city. It exhibits some Arawak objects (three of which are original) that were discovered during excavations in the region of Mullet Bay.

After walking down Frontstreet with its innumerable shops, the **pier**, by **Wathey Square**, lapped by soothing waves, is a calming place to take advantage of a few minutes of relative tranquillity.

Great Salt Pond, located north of Philipsburg, was exploited up until 1949. Most of the salt extracted was exported to the United States and the industry provided employment to a great many residents of Saint Martin. The end of the industry caused a serious crisis, and many people, finding themselves without income, were obliged to emigrate to other islands and more prosperous nations. Today the marsh attracts a few curious visitors, but it is above all frequented by birds, notably herons.

In the easternmost part of the city is **Bobby's Marina**, crowded with boats that drop anchor here. Cruises to Saint Barts also depart from here. The road then continues southward to Pointe Blanche, where there is a cluster of hotels and restaurants.

Outside of Philipsburg

Although it occupies a smaller territory, Sint Maarten is more populous than Saint-Martin, and most of its residents live on the outskirts of Philipsburg. The number of modest cottages that seem to be barely clinging to their foundations in these outlying neighbourhoods is surprising. Contrasting with the splendid homes along the coast, these houses are often the refuge of young and more or less legal workers who have migrated to the island in the hopes of earning a living. Hurricane Luis caused tremendous damage to these areas and it is still evident that not all of those wounds have healed.

The road that climbs the hills north of Philipsburg travels through **Dutch Cul De Sac** and **St. Peters**, where cottages stand one next to the other, seemingly arranged to occupy available space to its maximum potential. Essentially residential areas, these neighbourhoods offer little of interest to visitors.

After skirting Great Salt Pond, the main road leads to **Madame Estate**. This is the site of the **Sint Maarten Zoo** *(Mon to Fri 9am to 6pm, Sat and Sun 10am to 6pm;* ☎*22.748)*, where various

The Arawaks

Like the other islands of the Lesser Antilles, Saint Martin was inhabited long ago by the Arawaks (see p 12). These Amerindians lived in a hierarchical society and had their own myths and religious beliefs. They were quite skilled, and fashioned stone objects for the practice of their religion, several of which have been found in the Greater and Lesser Antilles. Some objects have also been found during excavations carried out under unusual conditions.

The relics on display at the museum were found in the sixties during the pre-construction work for a hotel in Mullet Bay. The site foreman, having discovered a cave containing Arawak objects, alerted the Dutch authorities. The response was so long in coming that the foreman gave up waiting and instead of preserving the unique site, decided to use it as a septic tank. He may have saved a few bucks, but at what price? Only three statuettes survived. Since then, other excavations have been carried out on Saint Martin to learn more about the pre-Columbian peoples that lived on the island.

species of animals from the Caribbean and South America can be observed. A botanical garden has also been laid out here.

West of Philipsburg

The Simson Bay Lagoon begins about five kilometre west of Philipsburg; this is where most of the tourist activity on the Dutch side of the island takes place. The road is lined with comfortable hotels, some of which have been converted to "time-sharing" apartments, built near the airport and alongside beautiful beaches.

To reach the tourist village of Mullet Bay from Philipsburg or the airport, take the main road west.

Among these tourist locales is **Mullet Bay ★**. A town consisting of a string of hotels, restaurants, casinos and boutiques, it is the main centre of this part of the island. Guests of the surrounding hotels converge here to take advantage of the services and enjoy the holiday atmosphere and long sandy beaches (Maho Beach, Mullet Bay and Cupecoy Beach).

Hotel complexes are numerous in this section of the island, and while the beaches here are not the jewels of the island, they do satisfy those craving fine sand and inviting surf. **Maho Beach** and **Mullet Beach**, both lined with hotels and condos, are often swarming and it can be difficult at times even to find enough space to spread out a towel. These are above all places to soak in the festive atmosphere and to see and be seen. Maho Bay also attracts Boeing 747-watchers because the airport is located at one end of the beach.

A little out of the way and offering a similar ambiance, **Cupecoy Beach** is a band of golden sand hidden at the foot of cliffs. A pleasant and popular spot, this is not a refuge of solitude-seekers.

East of Philipsburg

Continuing eastward past Philipsburg, the road penetrates the interior and passes through modest, uncharming villages. Be attentive, though: along the road there are turn-offs for Guana Bay, Dawn Beach and Oyster Pond, where some attractive hotel complexes as well as magnificent beaches are to be found.

Leaving Philipsburg, take the main road east. Barely a few kilometres out of the city the road intersects a smaller road, which leads to Guana Bay.

Winding roads snake through the rolling hills of this region and modest wooden cottages gradually give way to lavish homes, a contrast that intensifies as you approach the ocean. **Guana Bay** is a pretty village of a few luxurious, sumptuous houses built on the hills overlooking blue-tinted waves. A little beach completes this inviting scene.

No road links Guana Bay and Dawn Beach directly. To reach Dawn Beach, backtrack to the main road, continue east and take the second turn-off toward the ocean.

An excellent road goes down the steep cliff and leads to a small public parking lot next to the magnificent **Dawn Beach ★**. You can settle down comfortably at one end of this lovely crescent of silky sand, where chairs and parasols can be rented. There is also a small bar-restaurant with long wooden tables for those who wish to take a break from their tanning session and quench their thirst. At the other end of the beach stands the Dawn Beach hotel complex (see p 135). You can reach Dawn Beach by water taxi from Oyster Pond for US$2.

Oyster Pond Bay ★★ has the particularity of being divided between France (Saint-Martin) and Holland (Sint Maarten), but passing from one side to the other is easy, since there is no border-station. This pretty bay is developed on both sides.

On the way down the steep road to the beach, you'll notice that Oyster Pond Bay is almost entirely surrounded by hills, with only a narrow passage linking it to the Atlantic Ocean so that it looks like a small lake. This stretch of water is naturally quite calm and thus perfect for mooring boats, and a marina has been built. A number of comfortable hotels accommodate the water sports enthusiasts who frequent the spot.

 OUTDOOR ACTIVITIES

  Scuba Diving and Snorkelling

Not far off the coast of Sint Maarten, coral reefs have developed where snorkellers can enjoy themselves whole-heartedly. Most of the island's diving sites are located on the Dutch side, and the best-known spots are situated just off Dawn Beach and Maho Bay. Other sites are interesting not for their coral but for their shipwrecks. Divers can go down to see the remains of the English vessel *HMS Proselyte*, which sank in 1801 off Great Bay, or the wreck of the tugboat in Mullet Bay. Schools of fish swim about in these skeletons.

Oceans Explorer: Simson Bay, ☎44-252, ≈44-357.

Dive Safari: Bobby's Marina, Philipsburg, ☎26-024.

 Sailing

The marina at Oyster Pond is the prime spot for watching beautiful sailboats rocking on the waves. Sailing trips are organized by:

Ulti-Mate: Oyster Pond; excursions: US$30 to US$65.

 Hiking

Cole Bay Hill, a small mountain west of Philipsburg, is a pleasant climb. The hike takes about an hour and leads to the summit where an observation deck looks out on a splendid panorama. Bring water and plan the trip for the morning when the sun is not too hot.

 ACCOMMODATIONS

Philipsburg

At the heart of the thriving city of Philipsburg, the **Horizon View Beach Hotel** *(US$100; ≈, ℛ, K; 39 Frontstreet, ☎32-120, ≈20-705)* rents small and somewhat gloomy apartments. The most comfortable of them also have a lovely view of the ocean. Though the hotel is located in the centre of the city's action, the rooms are quiet.

A stone's throw from the Horizon View Hotel stands the **Holland House Beach Hotel** *(US$140; K; Frontstreet; ☎22-572, ≈24-673)*, which also has a beachfront location. In the heart of the bustle os the town, it doesn't exactly have an idyllic location. Nonetheless, it is tidy-looking and a little more pleasant than its neighbour. The rooms are decent, too.

🛥️ The **Pasanggrahan Royal Guesthouse Hotel** *(US$128; ℜ, ⊗; Frontstreet, P.O. Box 151, ☎23-588, ⇆22-885)* is somewhat of an anomaly in Sint Maarten. Indeed, it has nothing in common with the ubiquitous modern high-rises, as the owners decided to opt for charm instead. The front lobby is set up in a lovely colonial-style residence, prettily adorned with antique furnishings, while the rooms themselves are housed in two beachfront buildings. The oldest of the two, also in the colonial style, comprises lovely rooms graced with attractive wooden shutters and rattan furniture. The second, newer building boasts a somewhat more modern decor and added comfort. In addition to its attractive layout, the hotel offers guests a friendly welcome, a waterfront restaurant and direct access to the beach. One small quibble: it is located on busy Frontstreet, although it is on one of the quieter stretches of this commercial thoroughfare.

The charming, old-fashioned six-storey pastel-coloured buildings of the **Great Bay Beach Hotel** *(US$200; ℜ, ≈, ≋, ⊘; Little Road Bay, ☎22-446, ⇆22-859)*, a large complex on the outskirts of Philipsburg, stand in a relatively quiet setting. Although the rooms are altogether decent and there is a pleasant sandy beach, the site itself is hardly enchanting.

Mullet Bay, Maho Beach and Cupecoy Beach

Boutiques, hotel complexes, bars, restaurants and casinos make Mullet Bay and the area around it the busiest tourist spot on the island. This built-up region welcomes a large number of visitors who come to relax and have fun. There's just one problem: the main runway of the Princess Juliana airport is right at the end of the beach, and the planes can be rather disruptive.

Over the last few years, several hotel complexes in this tourist zone have been converted into comfortable apartment buildings whose units are rented out according to the time-share formula (see p 61). Such places will be referred to as Private Clubs so as to distinguish them from regular establishments. Even if you do not wish to become a member, you may still be able to stay in some such clubs, since their apartments are occasionally available for rent. A number of them go for US$225 a night, but better deals are often to be had. Because they are private, we were unable to visit many of these establishments; thus can we only offer you a short description of the places in question.

Mary's Boon *(US$120; ⊗, ℜ, K; 117 Simson Bay Rd., ☎54-235, ⇝53-403)* is visible as you disembark from the airplane, as it is located beside the runway. While this of course is a major disadvantage, the hotel offers 14 tastefully decorated rooms that look directly onto a beautiful beach. Particular attention is paid to service, which is always friendly.

The **Atrium Resort** *(US$180; ≡, ≈, ℜ; Pelican Rd., ☎42-125, ⇝42-128)* is one of the elegant hotel complexes built on the shores of Simson Bay. Elegantly decorated, with fewer than 100 rooms, this is the perfect spot for peaceful relaxation. While the Atrium has no gym, its guests have access to the facilities of the Pelican Resort and Casino (see below).

The **Pelican Resort and Casino** *(US$200; ≈, ℜ, ≡; P.O. Box 431, Philipsburg, ☎42-503)* is outside of this tourist town, near Philipsburg. Its old-looking building, standing by the side of the road in a less than picturesque setting, does not look like much, but it does offer pleasant rooms.

Among the big hotels at the edge of this pretty white-sand bay rises the eight-storey **Maho Beach Hotel and Casino** *(US$235 everything incl.; ≈, ℜ, ≡; Maho Bay, ☎52-115, ⇝53-180)*. Every aspect of this hotel has been designed with the comfort of the guest in mind. Everything revolves around a huge pool in the centre of the complex: a bar where you can enjoy a drink while sitting in the water, tennis courts, and of course the casino. With its 400 rooms, there is nothing quaint about this place, but it does offer the utmost in comfort.

Two hotels once formed the heart of the holiday village that is Maho Beach: these are the aptly named Maho Beach Hotel and the **Royal Islander Club** *(Private Club; P.O. Box 2000, Philipsburg, ☎52-388, ⇝53-495)*. The latter is a multi-storey building that was built some years ago and now looks some-what outdated. It has been converted into a private club and stands right on a lovely fine-sand beach.

The **Royal Palm Beach Club** *(Private Club; ☎43-737)* is set along the road linking Mullet Bay to Baie Nettlé, on the French side.

Its modern high-rise buildings, whose parking lot was still under construction at the time of our visit, are right on the seaboard, giving some of the apartments an ocean view.

Nearby stands the **Cupecoy Beach Club** *(Private Club; ☎52-243)*, which has a quiet, remote setting in a vast, little-inhabited landscape. It is located a mere stone's throw from Cupecoy Beach.

The **Towers at Mullet Bay** *(Private Club, ☎53-069)* consists of several modern and somewhat sterile high-rises that lack charm. Though it is only a short distance from the beach, the only view it offers is that of fields stretching out to the horizon.

Little Bay

Next to Philipsburg lies Little Bay, a small cove with two hotels, slightly removed from the road, at the foot of sheer cliffs. The first of these establishments, the **Divi Little Bay Beach Resort** *(Private Club; ☎22-233)*, lies at the bottom of a winding road that leads down to the bay. Its tidy layout makes the lovely setting very pleasant. It comprises a series of multi-storey cottages right by the sea, allowing guests to take full advantage of the beautiful ocean blue stretching out into the distance.

By retracing your steps and continuing west, you will come to the second of the two establishments, the **Belair Beach Hotel** *(US$225; ≡, K, ℝ; P.O. Box 140, Philipsburg, ☎23-362, ⌐25-295)*. Built on a tiny patch of ground by the sea, it has a marvellous view of the water, while the road lies on the other. The building, which has seen better days, is really nothing special, but provides adequate accommodation for vacationers who have come to take advantage of the beach, which is unfortunately very small. Every room has a dining area and a kitchenette.

Oyster Pond

Part of Oyster Pond Bay is French and part is Dutch. This is why some prices are listed in French francs and others in

American dollars. **Don't forget: the area code for Sint Maarten is 599-5, and you must add 05.90 before numbers in Saint-Martin.**

Located near the bay, **Sol Hotel** *(3,500 F per week; ≡; Oyster Pond No. 38, 97150, ☎05.90.87.38.10, ≈05.90.87.32.23)* is a good place to stay in Oyster Pond. Housed in a white building that is well kept and perfectly charming with its lovely pastel balconies, the hotel offers guests suitably comfortable rooms.

Captain Oliver's *(660 F; ≡, ℜ; Oyster Pond, 97150, ☎05.90.87.40.26, ≈05.90.97.40.84)* is basically the heart of Oyster Pond, located on the shore of the bay on a lot adjoining the marina. Rooms are in small, well-kept pavilions and its restaurant, which looks out onto the bay, is a pleasant spot for relaxing and admiring sailboats heading out for a day on the waves.

⛵ **Soleil de Minuit** *(US$170; ≈, ≡, ℜ; ☎05.90.87.34.66, ≈05.90.87.33.70)* was built on a hillside from which a panoramic view of the bay is captured at a glance. It goes without saying that this is a place of perfect tranquillity. The hotel offers charming rooms decorated with rattan furniture. The large patio, with a pool at the centre, is an ideal spot for relaxing and enjoying the view of the bay and its port.

Not far from the marina, the **Colombus Hotel** *(980 F; ≡, ≈, ℜ; ☎05.90.87.42.52, ≈05.90.87.39.85)* consists of a few pink and turquoise buildings. While it is not luxurious, the establishment does offer comfortable, attractive rooms that are flanked by a pleasant balcony from which guests can admire the ocean.

Oyster Pond Bay ends in a strip of land washed by the waters of the bay on one side, and by the Caribbean Sea on the other. The **Oyster Pond Beach Hotel** *(US$170 bkfst incl.; ≈, ≡, ℜ; B.P. 239, Oyster Pond, ☎22.206, ≈25.695)* has taken full advantage of this setting with its extraordinary buildings. Guests staying here enjoy two panoramas, depending on whether they are at the front or back of the house. The rooms are very comfortable.

⛵ The **Mississippi** *(520 F; ≈, ≡, ℜ; Oyster Pond, 97150, ☎05.90.87.33.81, ≈05.90.87.33.52)* is located in the hills surrounding Oyster Pond Bay. The rooms, embellished with a pretty wooden terrace, look out over the bay, allowing guests to soak up the picturesque countryside. With the sea at its feet, and isolated from the bay, the hotel is far from the hustle and bustle of the marina.

The **Dawn Beach** *(US$280 all-inclusive;* ≈*,* ℛ*,* ≡*; B.P. 389, Oyster Pond,* ☎*22.929,* ⊷*24.421)* hotel was built on an exceptional site in a cove all to itself, beside a beautiful fine-sand beach studded with sea-grape trees. Its lovely wooden bungalows are spread throughout a vast garden, so guests are not at all crowded. Removed from the other hotel complexes, this is a real haven of tranquillity.

RESTAURANTS

Philipsburg

The largest concentration of fast-food restaurants on the island, including Kentucky Fried Chicken, Burger King and Pizza Hut, is found in Philipsburg, no doubt to serve the needs of travellers in a hurry. There are stalls downtown near the pier selling sausages, Mexican food and hamburgers, all of which must be eaten standing up. Those with more time, of course, can eat in one of the many restaurants in town. The tourist information booths can provide details about the local establishments, as well as give you with a few coupons offering reductions on drinks or meals.

The menu at **Ric's Place** *($-$$; 69 Frontstreet, just steps from Wathey Square,* ☎*26-050)* is hardly inventive, but the Tex-Mex restaurant is convenient for those seeking a few moment's respite. It serves hearty meals like burgers and *chili con carne*, and has a lovely ocean view.

Also facing the sea, the delightful **Reggae Café** *($$; Wathey Square)* has an unpretentious, relaxed ambiance and tables on two terraces (one on each floor) looking out on the surf. The lovely warm hues of the decor are striking.

A veritable oasis of peace, **Kangaroo Court** *($-$$; Hendrick Straat, ☎24-278)* has a magnificent interior courtyard adorned with a profusion of green plants, tables with parasols, and a fountain; indeed, the place offers patrons sanctuary from the never-ending bustle of Frontstreet. Another of the establishment's considerable assets: it is one of the few places where the menu does not feature burgers. Rather, it offers dishes prepared from healthy ingredients, such as quiches, salads and grilled-chicken sandwiches. In short, a pleasant eatery where you can enjoy a good lunch before resuming your shopping.

Continuing along Frontstreet, you'll come to Bobby's Marina, across from which stands the **Greenhouse** *($$)*. Set back from bustling Frontstreet, this place offers much calmer surroundings. The menu is not very complicated: tuna salad, sandwiches and hamburgers. The charm of the Greenhouse lies mainly in its simple friendly atmosphere, perfect for a meal with friends.

Looking for good, simple, inexpensive French dining? **La Riviera** *($$$; 16 Frontstreet)* is the answer. The menu is always satisfying, the carefully-prepared dishes never disappointing. This is no-fuss bistro dining at its best.

The little hotel **Pasanggrahan** *($$-$$$; Frontstreet)* (see p 131) has a good restaurant that looks out directly on the sea. In a relaxed, unpretentious ambience, it serves a variety of simple, quality dishes, notably fried squid and grilled lamb chops .

One of the best restaurants in Philipsburg, **L'Escargot** *($$$-$$$$; Frontstreet)* has been prosperous and highly respected for no fewer than 25 years. The elegant dining room has no doubt contributed to its success, but it is above all the cuisine, especially the escargots, that charms its many diners.

One of Philipsburg's finest restaurants, the **Bec Fin** *($$$-$$$$; 141 Frontstreet, ☎22-976)*, prepares excellent meals featuring lots of fish and shellfish. The traditional French cuisine will satisfy most tastes.

Another spot to keep in mind in Philipsburg is **Antoine** *($$$-$$$$; 119 Frontstreet, ☎22-964)*, where succulent French and Creole specialties are concocted. Among the best-known dishes of the house is the lobster, always exquisitely presented. Excellent meat and poultry are among the other savoury selections. In addition to a delicious meal, guests enjoy a lovely view of the ocean from the dining room. The restaurant also serves good lunches *($$-$$$)*.

Mullet Bay, Maho Beach and Cupecoy Beach

Right in the heart of the tourist village is **Cheri's Café** *($$)*. With its carefree atmosphere, this place couldn't be friendlier and is always hopping. Crowds of people fill its outdoor terrace to enjoy a good meal and a good time. There is a bit of everything on the menu, from hamburgers to seafood.

The **Rumboat** *($$$)*, set up in a quaint building facing the street, is among the other noteworthy restaurants in the village. The menu, without being too sophisticated, does include a few good dishes of grilled fish and seafood.

Located between Philipsburg and Maho Reef, **The Globe** *($$-$$$; Airport Road, ☎42-236)* is a charming roadside restaurant worth keeping in mind. Good, reasonably priced dishes are prepared here. Among these are a few Mexican specialties, such as enchiladas and burritos, as well as a fine variety of dishes including steak, burgers and the daily specials, always served in generous portions. What's more, the decor is pleasant and the service courteous.

Oyster Pond

Many hotels have been built on the shores of Oyster Pond Bay. Many of these have restaurants, a few of which offer elaborate menus. The restaurant at the luxurious **Oyster Pond Hotel** *($$-$$$)* offers the choice between club sandwiches and some simple fish dishes.

There are, however, a few interesting spots in Oyster Pond, such as the restaurant at the hotel **Captain Oliver's** *($$-$$$)*. The dining room is particularly pleasant at noontime as it looks out over the sea and the marina. Although the view is the main reason to come here, the food, while not extravagant, is palatable. Salads and sandwiches are featured on the lunch menu.

The restaurant of the hotel **Mississippi** *($$$)* is pleasantly perched on a hillside. Guests enjoy a very beautiful setting while savouring simple but delicious dishes such as grilled steak or crab salad.

ENTERTAINMENT

Philipsburg

Philipsburg is buzzing with activity during the day and though it attracts fewer visitors at night, there are still a few interesting bars.

In the midst of the Frontstreet bustle is an outstanding establishment, the seaside **Reggae Café** *(Wathey Square)*. It is just the place to have a drink in a friendly, laid-back ambiance.

The **Greenhouse** *(Bobby's Marina)* looks out onto the marina and welcomes patrons for a meal or just a drink. You can also come to shoot some pool on one of the tables. The atmosphere is laid-back and friendly.

Mullet Bay

Cheri's Café is a huge outdoor bar set right in the middle of the tourist village. This is a great place from which check to out the action of the village while enjoying a drink. There is dancing as well.

Casinos

Though there are casinos only on the Dutch side of the island, no less than a dozen occupy this small territory. Many of the hotels on the French side have free shuttle services for high-rolling guests looking for a little lady luck.

The biggest is the **Casino Royale**, located at the Maho Beach Hotel. You can try your luck at one of the 19 blackjack tables, six American roulette tables or two French ones, or get rid of your small change in one of the 250 slot machines.

The **Atlantis Casino** *(Cupecoy Bay)* welcomes guests into a sublimely decorated room. Once again there are baccarat, blackjack and poker (Caribbean stud poker), craps and roulette tables, as well as slot machines.

The other casinos, the **Casino International** *(Little Bay Hotel)* and the **Golden Casino** *(Great Bay Beach Hotel)*, both have blackjack and poker (Caribbean stud poker) tables, slot machines and more.

The **Rouge et Noir** casino is the place for high rollers looking for unlimited stakes, as are the **Diamond Casino** and **Paradise Plaza**. All have baccarat, blackjack and poker (Caribbean stud poker) tables, as well as slot machines. Some have a view of the sea.

Oyster Pond

To soak up the last rays of the sun in Oyster Pond, stop by **Captain Oliver's**. Its terrace, looking right out onto the bay, is the ideal spot from which to take in the dazzling sunset while sipping a drink and chatting.

 SHOPPING

The Dutch part of the island is a true paradise for shoppers, since nothing is taxed. Thus, shopping has become one of the most popular activities in Sint Maarten. Philipsburg is the best place to shop, and Fronstreet, its main street, is brimming with a jumble of upscale boutiques and affordable shops. Whether you're looking for jewellery, clothing or alcohol, take the time to compare the quality of the products at different places before settling on anything.

The shops do not close at noon on Sint Maarten.

Philipsburg

Clothing

Sint Maarten T-shirts are among visitors' favourite souvenirs. There is an overwhelming selection of these in many of the shops on Frontstreet.

For elegant fashions, the **Ashburry** luxury boutique is recommended.

Designer shops, such as **Liz Claiborne**, **Polo Ralph Lauren** and **Tommy Hilfiger**, have shops on Frontstreet that present some of their namesakes' most beautiful creations.

Accessories

For bags, belts, hats and other accessories, stroll over to the **Summer Times** and **Little Switzerland** shops.

Jewellery and Porcelain

For luxurious jewellery and accessories that never fail to please lovers of beautiful objects who are not afraid to loosen their purse strings, **Ashburry**, **Colombian Emerald** (fabulous precious stones), **Little Switzerland** and **Oro de Sol** are the places to visit.

For less extravagant jewellery, try **New Amsterdam**.

Other stores on Frontstreet have a reputation for selling gold and silver jewellery at prices that approach bargain levels. It requires a bit of digging and negotiating, but the finds are often worth the effort. Among these shops, **Mirage** and **Shivas** are two locations to keep in mind.

Miscellaneous Souvenirs

Looking for a colourful souvenir, gift jewellery or an amusing knick-knack? Satisfaction awaits at the **American West Indies Company** *(Frontstreet)* or at the charming **Greenwith** *(Frontstreet)* shop.

Fans of beautiful earthenware will find plenty of delightful items at the **Dutch Delft Blue Gallery** *(Frontstreet)*, which features very attractive pieces fashioned by Dutch artisans. Plates, curios, tiles and vases are just some of the objects you can purchase here.

Street vendors offer baubles and inexpensive souvenirs of all sorts.

Beauty Products

Many shops specialize in quality beauty products and, while there are not really any bargains to be found, the great selection on display merits a look. **Lipstick** and **Penha** on Frontstreet are good places to go.

Wines and Spirits

When it comes to affordable spirits, Sint Maarten is a small paradise for bargain-hunters. A few shops on Frontstreet are recommended, notably **Diamond**, **Rams** and **Caribbean Liquor and Tobacco**. There is also a **Caribbean Liquor and Tobacco** stand at Princess Juliana airport.

Saint Martin has only one typical liquor, Guanaberry, prepared from rum and a berry indigenous to the island. It is available on Frontstreet at a shop simply called **Guanaberry**.

Mullet Bay

Clothing

Many little shops in Mullet Bay offer attractive selections of bathing suits and beachwear, notably **Canicule** and **Beach Bum**.

Children are catered to at **Margie Magic** *(Plaza del Lago)*, which sells tasteful clothing.

Miscellaneous Souvenirs

The Design Factory *(Plaza del Lago)* offers a lovely collection of decorative objects and hordes of other little souvenirs that are sure to please.

Although one wouldn't think to come to Sint Maarten to buy African crafts, the shop **Nativa** *(Plaza del Lago)* displays a very beautiful collection of masks, cloth and statuettes from that continent.

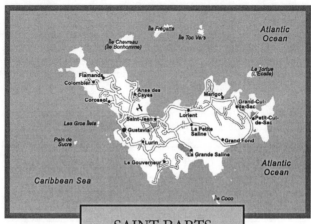

SAINT BARTS

A tour of the tiny islet of Saint Barts, with its mere 25 square kilometres of arid land, takes little time. And yet, it encompasses so many captivating landscapes, enchanting villages composed of charmingly Creole cottages and long, golden ribbons of sand bordered by azure waters, that visitors never tire of roaming its steep roads. Saint Barts is as small as it is beautiful, and each parcel of land is maintained with infinite care so that nothing should mar its beauty. This flower of the Caribbean is every bit as compelling as its neighbours.

 FINDING YOUR WAY AROUND

The island is criss-crossed by small, well-surfaced roads. A road passing by the airport links Gustavia to Saint-Jean. Another leads to Colombier, at the western extremity of the island. Yet another begins in Saint-Jean and goes through the eastern part of Saint Barts, passing through Lorient, Anse du Grand Cul-de-Sac, Anse Toiny and Grande Anse. This same road runs back to Saint-Jean. A junction also allows travellers to reach Gustavia. In certain places, a few roads lead to isolated coves, notably those of Grande Saline and Gouverneur.

Several car rental agencies have counters at the airport (see p 45), which is approximately two kilometres from Saint-Jean and Gustavia. Those who have rented a car or scooter should, upon leaving the parking lot, turn left to reach Saint-Jean, and right to reach Gustavia.

Travellers can also take a taxi, as there is a depot at the airport. Call ☎05.90.27.75.81 to reserve one.

 PRACTICAL INFORMATION

Banks

Banque Française Commerciale: Rue du Général de Gaulle, Gustavia, ☎05.90.27.62.62.

Crédit Agricole: Rue du Bord de Mer, Gustavia, ☎05.90.27.89.90.

Galerie du Commerce: facing the airport, Saint-Jean, ☎05.90.27.65.88.

Post Offices

At the corner of Rue du Centenaire and Rue Jeanne d'Arc, Gustavia, ☎05.90.27.62.00; Mon-Tue and Thu-Fri 8am to 5pm, Wed and Sat 8am to noon.

Galeries du Commerce, Saint-Jean, ☎05.90.27.64.02; Mon-Tue 8am to 2pm, Wed and Sat 7:30am to 11am.

Lorient, ☎05.90.27.61.35; Mon-Fri 7am to 11am, Sat 8am to 10am.

Medical Care

Hospital: ☎05.90.27.60.35

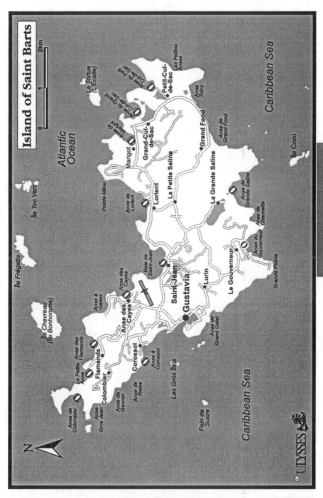

SAINT BARTS

Miscellaneous

Gendarmerie (inter-municipal police): ☎05.90.27.60.12
Police: ☎05.90.27.66.66
Weather: ☎05.90.27.60.17

SIGHTS AND BEACHES

Travellers following the paved road that winds its way through the island will soon come across some of its most resplendent treasures: Gustavia, Anse de Grand Fond, and Baie de Saint-Jean. To fully appreciate its charms, however, take the time to amble through its streets, to watch the frigate plowing through its choppy waters, to feel the trade winds, to contemplate the sea shimmering beneath the sun, to watch time pass. The following tour will allow you to discover the deepest reaches of Saint Barts.

Gustavia

The first colonists to settle on the island did so primarily to cultivate the land – a land whose sun-baked earth was the cause of much hardship. Saint Barts had a particular asset, however, in that it had a natural harbour, well-sheltered from sea currents and winds, and thus ideal for mooring boats. This geographic feature was extremely advantageous for this tiny island, as colonists were able to establish an excellent port, where the many vessels plying the Caribbean could find safe haven. The pirates who were then sailing the seas were among the first to benefit from the port, and would dock in the calm waters of the Carenage harbour. Their presence, though perilous, was nevertheless beneficial to the islanders, since this activity led to the gradual development of a city. However, the pirates who were despoiling foreign ships attracted the wrath of the great powers toward the residents of Saint Barts, and the expanding city was ultimately destroyed by the British in 1744.

Port Carenage, as it was then called, somehow managed to rise again from its ashes, and the city grew over the years. When Saint Barts was ceded to Sweden in 1785 in exchange for France's right to trade with that country, the island retained its importance, but was renamed **"Gustavia"** ★★★ in honour of the Swedish king who reigned at the time. It prospered under the Swedes, and new buildings with a very different architecture were constructed. Unfortunately, few buildings from this period remain, having been destroyed by the fire that ravaged

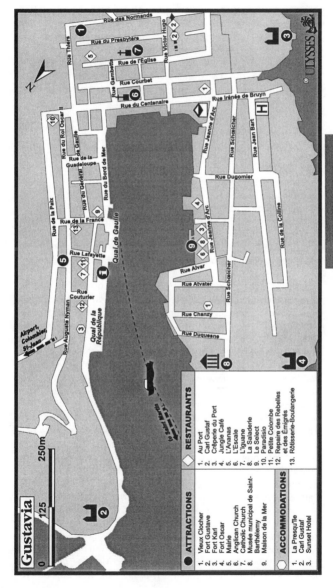

the island in 1852. The pretty green **Vieux Clocher**, or old bell tower, still stands on Rue du Presbytère. It once housed a bell cast in 1799, which rang off the important moments of the day. A clock has since replaced the bell.

At the end of the 18th and beginning of the 19th century, three forts were also built on the summits of the surrounding hills to protect the Swedish colony. The fortifications of only one of these 18th-century stone forts, **Fort Gustave**, can be viewed today. Visitors will find a terrace offering a lovely **view** ★ of Gustavia. Nothing remains of **Fort Karl**, while the fortifications of **Fort Oscar** have been modified over the years. This last site can only be observed from afar, as it is now occupied by the Minister of Armed Forces.

When France retook possession of the island in 1878, Gustavia kept its name and its status as the principal town on the island, and the residents remained exempt from taxes. It is still the busiest and largest urban area in Saint Barts. If you arrive by boat, you will find yourself more or less in the centre of town.

It is worth exploring the few streets radiating outward from the harbour, all lined with pretty little white houses topped by orange roofs. Wander about and explore Gustavia's charming back streets, enjoy its cafes and good restaurants, or give in to temptation and browse through its many shops. Besides the quaint houses, there are some distinguished edifices, like the **Mairie** (town hall) *(Rue Auguste Nyman)*, also called the *Maison du Gouverneur*, or governor's house, since the island's governors used to reside here. The stone foundation of this house supports a lovely green and white façade. Two other buildings are also worth a look. Built in 1885 of stone and wood, the **Anglican church** *(Rue du Centenaire)* is topped by a pretty bell tower. It still serves a sizeable congregation. The church is located on one of the prettiest streets in town, **Rue du Centenaire** ★, which runs along the port, providing a good view of Gustavia. Meanwhile, the austere white façade of the **Catholic church** *(Rue de L'Eglise)*, the more imposing of the two, is visible in the distance from Rue du Centenaire.

You could spend a day visiting Gustavia's sights. If you are curious about the history, traditions and daily life of Saint Barts, head to the **Musée Saint-Barthélemy** *(10 F; Mon to Thu 8am to noon and 1:30pm to 5:30pm, Fri until 5pm, Sat 8:30am to*

Anglican Church

noon; Wall House, corner of Alvar and Duquesne streets, **☎05.90.29.71.55)**, which exhibits various objects evocative of an earlier time, when the Swedes and French settled here.

The streets bordering the natural harbour are very lively, as they are lined with pleasant shops, restaurants, the marina and, of course, companies offering excursions at sea. Among these, the **Maison de la Mer ★** *(6 Rue Jeanne d'Arc,* **☎05.90.27.81.00)** provides an opportunity to explore the sea floor. Visitors can observe this fascinating world aboard the vessel *l'Aquarius*. Comfortably seated in the hull of the boat, passengers view the marine life through a glass dome.

Follow Rue Auguste Nyman out of Gustavia, past the airport and into Saint-Jean.

Saint-Jean

The town of **Saint-Jean ★** lies stretched along the shore of the beautiful Baie de Saint-Jean. At first it seems like a town that does not amount to much more than several shopping centres, most notably the Galeries du Commerce, the Villa Créole and the Centre Commercial Saint-Jean. However, visitors will soon discover that this village has some lovely houses. Decorated

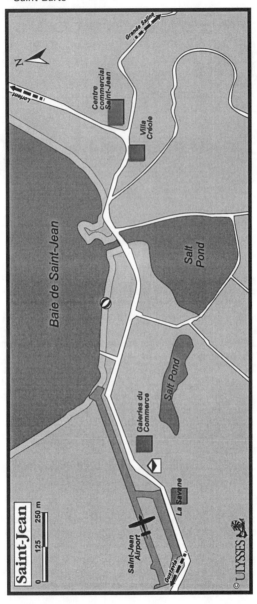

Saint-Jean

0   125   250 m

Baie de Saint-Jean

Grande Saline

Lorient

Centre commercial Saint-Jean

Villa Créole

Salt Pond

Salt Pond

Galeries du Commerce

La Savane

Saint-Jean Airport

Gustavia

© ULYSSES

with friezes and white balconies, they are built on the hillside and confer a great deal of charm to the village. Saint-Jean's main attraction is hidden behind lush vegetation: the **Baie de Saint-Jean** ★★, whose shimmering turquoise waters wash up onto a long crescent of golden sand. This virtual paradise attracts a busy crowd of sun worshippers and swimmers (park your car on the side of the road). However, this is hardly a noisy, bustling city, but rather a pleasant place where an atmosphere of peace and tranquillity reigns. Many people are also drawn by the considerable number of comfortable hotels standing at the water's edge (see p 162). In addition to the superb beach, there are the many fine restaurants along the waterfront to be enjoyed in between swims (see p 172).

Continue toward Lorient.

Lorient

Though the route to **Lorient** follows the sea, all that is visible from the road is the vegetation surrounding the resort complexes and pretty residences. In certain places the road opens up onto beautiful views of the precipitous coastline plunging into the sea. On your way into the village, you'll pass a grocery store, then a little cemetery whose tombstones are adorned with plastic flowers. This cute little hamlet lies on the shores of **Anse de Lorient** ★, a beautiful, fine-sand-covered beach sure to please surfing enthusiasts.

The road continues east to a less populated area of the island, making a loop as it passes by the beautiful beaches of Anse du Grand Cul-de-Sac, Petit Cul-de-Sac and the magnificent southeastern coast.

Pointe Milou

This part of the island is dominated by sheer cliffs to which magnificent homes cling, benefitting from an unobstructed view of the choppy waters below. The place is quite secluded and perfectly quiet. A stroll through this fashionable district of Saint Barts will certainly prove relaxing, but be forewarned, there are

SAINT BARTS

strong gusts of wind and visitors should refrain from touring the area on a moped.

Grand and Petit Cul-de-Sac

The eastern extremity of the island is on the windward coast. It is punctuated by intensely blue lagoons that lie at the bottom of sheer cliffs, well-sheltered from the wind and strong currents. Among these lagoons is the **Anse du Grand Cul-de-Sac** ★★, a beautiful cove where quaint orange-roofed houses are reflected in the crystal-clear waters, girdled by cliffs, making it a haven for windsurfing buffs and swimmers alike. Certain hoteliers have also wished to take advantage of this exceptional spot, and lovely hotel complexes have been built here. Nevertheless, the area remains peaceful and not overly frequented.

Just a few steps from Grand Cul-de-Sac, nestled at the base of the hills, is the **Anse de Marigot**. Steep cliffs rise up all around this lagoon, protecting it from the wind and making it a popular spot with both swimmers and small-boat owners, who moor their crafts in its calm waters.

East of Anse du Grand Cul-de-Sac, **Anse du Petit Cul-de-Sac** is even less developed. The undergrowth and sea-grape trees growing here and there provide welcome shade from the hot sun and create the feeling of a deserted beach. Anse du Petit Cul-de-Sac has all the charm of a typical Caribbean beach far from the towns and free of any touristy developments. No construction blots its landscape because the beach is covered in rocks of all sizes, making it impossible to swim there.

Anse Toiny and Anse Grand Fond

As the road continues, the landscape changes, with beaches of fine sand gradually giving way to steep cliffs. There are no fine-sand beaches in the southeastern part of the island; **Anse Toiny** and **Anse Grand Fond** ★★ are bordered by sheer walls of rock continuously slammed by waves. The wild scene is rendered almost hypnotic by the huge, peaceful expanse of blue sea, only occasionally broken by a colourful boat going by. If you

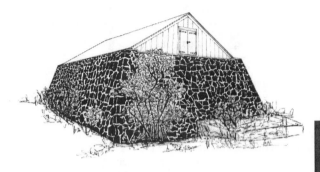

Cabrette

like rugged scenery, then take the time to visit this unspoilt region.

Alert travellers can catch sight of a typical Saint-Barts cottage, the *cabrette*, on the left side of the road, a little past the superb Le Toiny hotel (see p 167). A very low, small stone cottage, it was built to resist the wind's worst onslaughts.

The road follows the shore from Anse Toiny all the way to Anse Grand Fond before cutting inland. It snakes through the hills, climbs abruptly at times, then zigzags downhill between beautiful residences. Touring this part of the island by bike requires a lot of stamina. The region is sprinkled with charming little houses adorned with friezes and tiny gardens where rare cultivated island plants do their best to grow and flower. Dreamy and peaceful, this area typifies Saint Barts perhaps more than any other.

In Petite Saline, the road splits in two, with one fork heading to Lorient and the other continuing inland; take the latter (keep left) and drive another kilometre, at most, to another fork; keep left to reach Anse de Grande Saline.

Anse de Grande Saline

Before reaching the ocean, you'll cross the interior and come upon the huge white rectangle formed by the cloudy water of the Grande Saline. In the past, salt was extracted from this saltern, endowing some residents of Saint Barts with substantial returns. The Grande Saline is surrounded by a mangrove swamp and attracts many species of birds (especially waders), which can be observed by anyone with a pair of binoculars. This saltern lends its name to the beach located right next to it, **Anse de Grande Saline ★★**. Next to the swamp is a parking lot where visitors can leave their cars. A short path must then be taken, at the end of which a marvellous tableau awaits you: the azure ocean as far as the eye can see, and not a building in sight. This beach is renowned for its wild beauty, the lush green hills surrounding it, its fine sand and crystal-clear waters. Far different from such touristy beaches as Baie de Saint-Jean, it is incomparably beautiful, its natural surroundings still untouched by any kind of development. Those who enjoy quiet swims and soft sand will be particularly contented.

To reach Gouverneur beach, retrace your steps toward Gustavia. In Lurin, a little village in the hills comprising a few cottages, you can take the road leading back down to the beach. Drivers should pay attention, however, for the road is badly marked; it is right next to the France Telecom buildings.

Anse du Gouverneur

The road goes down to the ocean, passing by small houses set in the middle of vast plots of land. Rather unpopulated, this rural region is strewn with somewhat wild vegetation. The road ends next to the vast property of a private residence, and visitors will have to leave their vehicles in the tiny parking lot or, as it is often full, on the side of the road. A very short path leads to the beautiful golden beach of the **Anse du Gouverneur ★★**, where gently lapping waves make swimming so inviting. No businesses blot the landscape of this wonderfully quiet cove, where only a single private dwelling borders the beach. With no merchants or parasol-renting kiosks (those with sensitive skin should provide for their own shelter), this beach is the quintessential small, forgotten Caribbean paradise.

To visit the western part of the island, travellers must return to Gustavia. A few typical cottages line the road winding through the hills. From the top of these, looking down into the valley, you will see Gustavia: a multitude of orange roofs radiating out from the harbour, where all sorts of boats are moored.

To get to Corossol, retrace your steps and turn left on the first road you come across. This road leads to Gustavia, from where it continues to Corossol.

Corossol

Corossol ★ is a tiny community that has developed on a hillside at the edge of **Anse de Corossol**. Here again, quaint little orange-roofed houses elegantly decorated with friezes brighten up an otherwise drab landscape of shrubs and undergrowth. This modest, typically Caribbean village has a certain charm, and fortunately the road running alongside the pretty beach gets little traffic. This is a wonderful place to unwind on sunny days, when colourful fishing boats bob in the water off in the distance, and the odd pelican glides by.

A small museum called the **Inter Ocean Museum ★** *(20 F; Tue to Sun 9:30am to 5pm; ☎05.90.27.62.97)* has opened here. It displays all kinds of shells (more than 400 varieties). This unique treasure was collected by the owner, M. Magras, over his lifetime.

To reach the centre of the island and the village of Colombier, return to the main road and turn left at the first intersection.

Colombier

This hamlet, high in the hills in the western part of the island, has been isolated for many years even though it is only two kilometres from Gustavia. Farmers in these parts had to work hard to reap meagre livelihoods from their unproductive lands. In 1918, Père De Bruyn wanted to help these poor people, and

SAINT BARTS

thanks to his efforts a chapel, school and water tank were built. The chapel still stands at the centre of the village. Colombier enjoys a superb view from its perch up in the hills, where the land rolls away into the rippling waves of the sea.

At its very tip, you will find a path leading to **Grand Colombier** ★★ beach, the last one at this extremity of the island. A fifteen-minute walk through some small shrubs will lead you to this beach, the most isolated on Saint Barts. Once again, you will be enthralled by the quality of its sand, as fine as it is soft, bordering the crystal-clear waters. This unparalleled tableau is yet another of the rapturous treasures of the magnificent islet that is Saint Barts. Save some drinking water for the trek back to the parking lot, because you will have to climb uphill all the way back.

Head back down the northern coast of the island; you will arrive at Anse des Flamands.

Anse des Flamands

Anse des Flamands ★ is the most westerly beach on the island. It curves into a long crescent of white sand, and is dotted here and there by latania, trees whose large palm leaves are used to make hats and baskets. The peace and quiet of this beach make it an ideal spot for swimming and enjoying a siesta in the shade of a latania tree.

Anse des Cayes

Not far from Baie de Saint-Jean, **Anse des Cayes** has acquired quite a reputation for surfing. Those who dream only of sunbathing will also find its fine sand to their liking.

 OUTDOOR ACTIVITIES

With its 22 fine-sand beaches stretching along the Caribbean Sea and the Atlantic Ocean, Saint Barts is a real paradise for water-sports enthusiasts. In fact, most of the island's outdoor activities are water sports. Besides enjoying the surf, however, you can go horseback riding and bicycling.

Swimming

If swimming is your thing, then you are all set, you just have to pick the spot. Of the island's 22 beaches, 15 are great for swimming, and each is prettier than the last. The quality of the water at all of these beaches is monitored every year and found to be excellent (except at Gustavia, where it is average).

Beaches on the island are divided into two groups: those on the windward side, or *Côte au Vent*, and those on the leeward side, or *Côte sous le Vent*. Worth mentioning among the first are the beaches on Baie St-Jean, Anse Lorient, Grand and Petit Cul-de-Sac, Anse Toiny and Anse de Grande Saline; these beaches are usually pounded by rough surf, although some are protected by natural breakwaters. The second group, includes the beaches of Anse Corossol, Anse Colombier, Anse des Flamands and Anse des Cayes; unlike the former, these beaches are usually calm. Finally, take note that there are no nudist beaches on Saint Barts.

For sanitary reasons dogs are not permitted on beaches.

Scuba Diving

The warm waters along the island's coasts provide an ideal environment for the development of coral, which in turn attracts all sorts of tropical fish. Droves of diving enthusiasts come here to witness this vivid underwater spectacle. There are many interesting sites to explore, such as the sea bottom and coral reefs off the beaches at Anse Chauvette, Anse Corossol, and Île de la Tortue. Excursions are also offered to the island of Tintamarre (Saint Martin) and Saba (Dutch Antilles; for experienced divers only). These expeditions include a boat trip and a picnic. It costs an average of about 300 F per dive, and 450 F to 500 F for a novice's first dive.

The following centres organize diving excursions:

St-Barth Plongée: Port of Gustavia, ☎05.90.27.54.44.

West Indies Dive: Marine Service, Quai du Yacht, Gustavia, ☎05.90.27.70.34.

Mermaid Diving Centre: Hotel St. Barth Beach, ☎05.90.58.79.29.

Ocean Must: Rue Alvar, beside the museum, ☎05.90.27.62.25.

 Snorkelling

The ocean depths boast magnificent natural scenery for those who dare venture underwater. If you are curious but do not wish to go scuba diving, renting snorkelling gear is an option:

Snorkelling Marina: Gustavia, ☎05.90.27.96.68.

Wind Wave Power: Anse du Grand Cul-de-Sac, ☎05.90.27.82.57.

Hookipa: equipment; Gustavia, ☎05.90.27.76.17.

Hookipa: equipment; Saint-Jean, ☎05.90.27.71.31.

 Cruises

Excursions aboard sailboats and yachts are an enchanting way to explore the sea's sparkling waves. Some centres organize excursions.

Marine Services: Gustavia Pier, ☎05.90.27.70.34.

St. Barth Caraïbes Yachting: Quai de Gustavia, ☎05.90.27.52.48.

Ocean Must: Quai de Gustavia, ☎05.90.27.62.25.

Windsurfing

The relatively quiet beaches of Grand Cul-de-Sac and Anse Saint-Jean, or the more exciting ones in Lorient, are particularly appreciated by sailboarders. Some enterprises along these beaches rent the necessary gear and offer lessons (rentals cost about 130 F per hour):

Wind Wave Power: Grand Cul-de-Sac, ☎05.90.27.82 57.

St-Barth Wind School: Saint-Jean, ☎05.90.27.71.22.

Mermaid Diving Centre: Anse du Grand Cul-de-Sac.

 Surfing

The Lorient beach is often battered by strong waves, making it an ideal place to surf. Intrepid surfers who have mastered their technique will enjoy Anse Toiny and its swelling seas.

Hookipa: Saint-Jean, ☎05.90.27.67.63.

Saint-Barth Sports Agency: Lorient, ☎05.90.27.68.06.

 Water-skiing

If you are in the mood to skim across the waves at high speeds, then water-skiing is for you. Mastering this activity does require some experience, but with a little patience and some good advice you should get the hang of it.

Marine Service: Gustavia Pier, ☎05.90.27.70.34.

 Jet-skiing

If you get the urge to careen across the waves at full tilt, head to Anse du Grand Cul-de-Sac where you can rent these water-bound rockets for 300F per half hour.

Mermaid Diving Centre: Anse du Grand Cul-de-Sac.

Deep-sea Fishing

Deep-sea fishing excursions not only offer the excitement of a big catch on the high seas, but also make for a fun outing. These trips usually last half a day. Equipment and fishing advice are provided.

Marine Service: Gustavia Pier, ☎05.90.27.70.36.

Ocean Must: Quai de Gustavia, ☎05.90.27.62.25.

Hiking

At the centre of tiny Saint Barts, you'll find steep hills covered only with undergrowth and shrubs. Several roads run across these hills, but there are few hiking trails. Presently, there is only one in the region of Colombier. If you head off on a trek, make sure you are well equipped (good walking shoes, light-coloured clothing and food) and well-protected from the sun (sunscreen, sunglasses and a hat) to avoid sunstroke; leave early in the morning with plenty of food and water.

Bicycling

The island is criss-crossed by narrow roads that are often very steep and offer little shade. It is therefore not the ideal place for bicycling. However, a bicycle can be very useful for short distances. Rentals are available in several different spots.

Ouanalao Moto: Galeries du Commerce, Saint-Jean, ☎05.90.27.88.74.

Chez Béranger: Gustavia, ☎05.90.27.89.00.

A lone sailboat moored in Gustavia harbour, Saint Barts.
- *Claude-Hervé Bazin*

This fisherman's boat shows off its lovely blue and red colours on the calm waters at the port of Corossol.
- *L.P.*

Creole houses on Saint Barts display fine architectural detail, such as this one with its wood trim. - *L.P.*

A pretty Creole house on Saint Barts surrounded by a magnificent garden. - *L.P.*

Horseback Riding

A riding stable near Baie des Flamands organizes excursions on horseback. This is a pleasant way to discover another side of the island.

Ranch des Flamands: Baie des Flamands, ☎05.90.27.80.72.

 ACCOMMODATIONS

Saint Barts offers an incomparable choice of fine luxury hotels, with facilities to satisfy your every need. Staying on the cheap, however, can be quite a challenge; the French bed and breakfast association, the *Gîtes de France*, has no members on the island, and there are few budget hotels.

We have listed what we believe to be the best accommodations, keeping in mind the price category, location and particular advantages of each one.

Gustavia

The pretty town of Gustavia, with its shops, restaurants and marina, is always busy with visitors strolling about. With much to see and do, it is a pleasant place to pass the day, but there isn't much reason to spend the night, when the beaches and hills surrounding the city are so much more pleasant. There are only two hotels in the centre of town. One of these, the **Presqu'île** *(330 F; ≡, tv; Place de la Parade, Gustavia 97133, ☎05.90.27.64.60, ⊷05.90.27.72.30)*, faces the marina and rents out a few basic rooms. This isn't a dream hotel, but it is well worth the affordable price.

The second hotel in the centre of Gustavia is the three-storey **Sunset Hotel** *(600 F; ≡, tv; Rue de la République, B.P. 102, Gustavia 97133, ☎05.90.27.77.21, ⊷05.90.27.81.59)*, which also faces the marina. The rooms are well kept and more comfortable than the Presqu'île's, ensuring a good night's sleep.

The **Carl Gustaf** *(3,500 F bkfst incl.; ≈, ≡, ℛ, K; Rue des Normands, Gustavia 97133, ☎05.90.27.82.83, ⇒05.90.27.82.37)* comprises a series of luxury villas built on a hillside away from the downtown area. Each villa has an exceptional view of the town's streets and the crystalline waves of the sea. To make the most of this superb location, each villa has a lovely terrace looking out over the beautiful landscape. These units are extremely comfortable and feature a small private pool and nicely-decorated rooms with big picture windows that frame the sea.

Saint-Jean

Saint-Jean is the second largest-town after Gustavia. The centre of the village proper actually consists of just a few small houses. All around, beautiful fine sand beaches unfold, lined by hotels built to take full advantage of this superb location. The hotels are easy to find since most are clustered together along the main road; each one, however, has its own vast property to provide guests with a measure of privacy.

The **Hôtel Émeraude Plage** *(1,050 F; ≡, ⊛, ℛ, K; Baie de Saint-Jean 97133, ☎05.90.27.64.78, ⇒05.90.27.83.08)* stands in the midst of a huge garden facing Baie de Saint-Jean; it therefore boasts a delightfully peaceful setting and direct access to the beach. No fewer than 24 bungalows (some accommodating up to four people) are spread out on either side of the garden, all with a view of the sea. They are all functional (each has an equipped kitchen) and very comfortable, without being too luxurious.

🦐 The pretty villas of the **Filao Beach Hotel** *(1,900 F garden view, 2,700 F sea view; ≡, ⊛, tv, K; B.P. 667, Saint-Jean 97099, ☎05.90.27.64.84, ⇒05.90.27.62.24)*, a member of the prestigious *Relais et Châteaux* association, lie nearby. They are surrounded by a pleasant garden planted with trees and bushes of all kinds, ideal for strolling about and observing all the activity around the bird feeder. At the far end, you'll find a beautiful golden beach and the shimmering sea. You can drink in this beautiful sight while enjoying a meal on the hotel's terrace. This oasis of tranquillity is the perfect place for a relaxing, restful vacation.

The **Tropical Hotel** *(1,080 F garden view, 1,230 F sea view; ≈, ≡, ⊛, tv; B.P. 147, Saint-Jean 97095, ☎05.90.27.64.87, ⊷05.90.27.81.74)* is built on a hillside. To get there, take the road on your right on your way from Marigot (a sign indicates the way). The ideally-located buildings offer an exceptional view of the blue sea stretched out below. The charming well-maintained rooms are decorated with rattan furniture. Unfortunately, the hotel is not right on the beach, though a lovely pool makes up for this small drawback.

🏨 The **Village St. Jean** *(1,000 F bkfst incl.; ≈, ⊛; 97133, ☎05.90.27.61.39, ⊷05.90.27.77.96)* is another comfortable establishment, nestled in the hills above Baie de Saint-Jean. It comprises several bungalows, attractively decorated with woodwork, spread out over a vast property. All have very lovely rooms, also adorned with attractive wood panelling. These rooms are airy and very simply furnished, but have an undeniable charm. In addition to enjoying the magnificent panorama, guests can take a luxurious dip in the large, tranquil swimming pool.

For a pleasant stay in a relaxed atmosphere, **Eden Rock** *(3,700 F for a room, 4,680 for a suite, all have ocean views; ℜ; 97133, ☎05.90.27.72.94, ⊷05.90.27.88.37)* is the place. It is reached, with some difficulty, via a steep dirt road that climbs the hillside. The rooms are located in colourful buildings, some of which are located at the top of the hill, surrounded by a profusion of plants. The view from here is exquisite. The other rooms are located in beachfront buildings. Particular attention has been given to the decoration of the rooms; each has individual flair accented with antique furniture and lace curtains.

The **Tom Beach** *(1,800 F; ≈, ≡; 97133, ☎05.90.27.53.13, ⊷05.90.27.53.15)* has undeniably charming colonial-style rooms, furnished with a special attention to detail and pleasant touches like magnificent canopied four-poster beds, beamed ceilings and shuttered windows. The rooms are scattered throughout a smallish garden, where an abundance of flowering plants grow all the way down to the beautiful Saint-Jean beach.

Lorient

By following the main road, you'll come upon Lorient, a small hamlet with just a few houses. The beach of Anse Lorient and the charming hotels lie nearby.

La Normandie *(350 to 450 F; ≈, ≡; 97133, ☎05.90.27.61.66, ⌐05.90.27.98.83)* is located by the road, in a less than enchanting setting. It does, however, offer reasonably-priced rooms, which are well-maintained and quite comfortable, though hardly charming. The establishment also boasts a little garden with a small swimming pool.

🦑 The **Manoir de Saint-Barthélemy** *(400 to 650 F; ≈, K; 97133, ☎05.90.27.79.27, ⌐05.90.27.65.75)* is surely unique in Saint Barts. In a vast and magnificent garden lies a 17th-century Breton manor that was transported to the island and rebuilt beam by beam; this building houses the hotel's main hall. The rooms are fitted out in wooden bungalows whose architecture echoes that of the manor. They are very large and magnificently decorated with tastefully-chosen antique furniture. The bed, for instance, is draped in a white mosquito net, giving it the romantic appearance of yesteryear. A feeling of well-being emanates from these rooms, and the meticulous attention to detail at this establishment – one without equal in Saint Barts – is a real treat. And for the price, it is truly a bargain.

Travellers can rent one of the small white cottages from the **Les Mouettes** *(700 F; ⊛, K; 97133, ☎05.90.27.77.91, ⌐05.90.27.68.19)* establishment, whose property goes right down to the ocean's blue waters. Each villa is equipped with a balcony overlooking the sea, a simple yet lovely decor and a kitchenette. Moreover, the beach's proximity makes the place a great vacation spot.

The rooms of the **Hôtel La Banane** *(1,400 F bkfst incl.; ≈, ℛ, ≡; Lorient 97133, ☎05.90.27.68.25, ⌐05.90.27.68.44)* are all set up inside pretty, colonial-style Creole houses, giving the hotel a special character. The shutters, wooden walls and rustic, old-fashioned furniture fit right in, lending the place a comfortable, homey feel.

Around Lorient

The **Hostellerie des 3 Forces** *(840 F; ≈, ≈, ⊗, ℛ; Vitet, 97133,* ☎*05.90.27.61.25,* ⊷*05.90.27.81.38)* is a friendly establishment built right in the mountains, in very quiet surroundings. The rooms are in lovely wooden cottages, fitted out with balconies whence guests can contemplate their surroundings. They are simply furnished, but comfortable. To reach the hotel, follow the signs from Lorient.

Pointe Milou

Past Lorient, the road winds along the hillside with signs leading to Pointe Milou. This road is very steep and seems to lead nowhere, but don't despair; upon reaching the bottom of the cliff you will come upon the beautiful buildings of the **Christopher Hotel** *(2,500 F; ≈, ≈, ℛ; B.P. 571, 97098,* ☎*27.63.63,* ⊷*27.92.92)*. The site consists of a series of oceanfront buildings terraced into the cliff side. The rooms are impeccably maintained and adorned with wooden furnishings. Each of them has a large terrace overlooking the sea and a lovely bathroom. Though the beach is somewhat rocky, the site itself is pleasantly laid out, with a huge private terrace and a magnificent swimming pool at guests' disposal.

Anse de Marigot

There is a small beach along the shores of Anse de Marigot. Just beside it, however, is the beautiful beach of Anse du Grand Cul-de-Sac. This explains the lack of hotels along Anse de Marigot. The **Sea Horse Hotel** *(1,050 F; ≈, ≈, K; Anse de Marigot 97133,* ☎*05.90.27.85.33,* ⊷*05.90.27.75.36)* was built on the cliffs facing Anse de Marigot, and thus enjoys an exceptionally peaceful setting. Although it is a bit far from the ocean, the buildings were designed so that each room has a balcony overlooking the glittering waves. All of the suites have kitchenettes, and for those with a craving for grilled food, barbecues are provided on a rooftop terrace. The place also rents out 10 studios with kitchenettes, parking and terraces overlooking the sea for 1,500 F.

Grand Cul-de-Sac

The beach at Anse du Grand Cul-de-Sac is the prettiest in this part of the island, and several hotels have been built here to take advantage of this beautiful, isolated crescent of golden sand. Far from all the hustle and bustle, this beach is a real vacation paradise.

Résidence du Bois l'Angélique *(750 F; ≈, ≡, ⊗, K; 97133, ☎05.90.27.92.82, ⌐05.90.27.96.69)* has been designed so that guests can benefit from a splendid view of the silvery waters of Anse du Grand Cul-de-Sac stretching out into the distance. Every room has a charming terrace opening out on this magnificent tableau. Each has a simple and airy decor, quite pleasant for those seeking shelter from the hot rays of the sun.

Pavilions, built in the heart of a charming garden, house the rooms of the **El Sereno** *(1,250 F bkfst incl. garden view, 1,500 F bkfst incl. sea view; ≡, ≈, tv, ℛ; B.P. 19, Grand Cul-de-Sac 97095, ☎05.90.27.64.80, ⌐05.90.27.75.47)*. Each is pleasantly decorated and has a terrace with rattan furniture looking out over the shady, verdant surroundings. The pool and restaurant are located on a terrace lookout overhanging the waves of Grand Cul-de-Sac. This wonderfully tranquil spot affords magnificent views of the seascape.

Though the garden of the **St. Barths Beach Hotel** *(1470F; ≈, ≡, ℛ, ℛ; B.P. 580, 97098, ☎05.90.27.60.70, ⌐05.90.27.77.59)* can hardly be described as superb, as it is practically non-existent, the beachfront buildings have a pleasant setting. Moreover, all the rooms have a little balcony overlooking the sea. The large, well-kept and simply decorated rooms offer decent comfort without being luxurious. The proximity of the sea lends the place a pleasant beach-vacation ambiance.

Near the St. Barths Beach Hotel, and part of the same hotel complex are the **Résidences Saint-Barth** *(1,170 F; ≡, ≈, ℛ, ⊘, K; B.P. 81, Petit Cul-de-Sac 97098, ☎05.90.27.85.93, ⌐05.90.27.77.59)*. Built on the hill overlooking the bay, the 21 one-, two- and three-room villas all have big bay windows and a pretty terrace from which to enjoy the stunning land-scape. No less than seven little pools are at guests' disposal.

🛥 Upon entering **Guanahani** *(2,280 F bkfst incl.; ≡, ≈, ⊗, tv, K; B.P. 609, Grand Cul-de-Sac 97098, ☎05.90.27.66.60, ⬝05.90.27.70.70)*, you will discover a beautiful lobby with dark floors and colourful walls, opening discreetly onto the sea. The charming villas, with their pretty white friezes and sky-blue doors, are located in a vast garden surrounding the main building. Each villa has a terrace, and the fancier ones have a private pool or a whirlpool bath. The sea unfurls at the far end of the garden.

Anse Toiny

🛥 Anse Toiny is located on the steepest shore of the island, and the rough surf makes swimming impossible. It was here, in front of the unbridled sea, that the owner of **Le Toiny** *(3,960 F; ≡, ≈, ⊗, tv, K, ℜ; Anse Toiny 97133, ☎05.90.27.88.88, ⬝05.90.27.89.30)* chose to build a luxurious hotel offering unparalleled comfort. Luxurious villas with magnificent wood floors, elegant furniture, and wonderfully bright, airy rooms make guests feel at home. Everything is impeccable, even the bathrooms. The best thing about these villas is that the rooms all open onto a terrace with a private pool. A cut above the rest, Le Toiny boasts an exceptionally peaceful setting.

Colombier

🛥 The adorable village of Colombier is located in the hills in the western part of the island. Erected on the outskirts of this peaceful village, the **François Plantation** *(1,500 F; ≡, ≈, tv, ℜ; Colombier 97133, ☎05.90.29.80.22, ⬝05.90.27.61.26)* hotel stands on a vast property planted with trees and flowering shrubs that offer welcome shade. At the heart of this verdant vegetation, you'll find a number of cozy, colourful bungalows. Some look out onto the garden, while the more expensive units afford a neverending view of the sea. You'll discover an oasis of serenity here.

🐚 Past Colombier, at the very end of the road, is **P'tit Morne** *(800 F; ≈, ⊛, K; 97096, ☎05.90.27.62.64, ⇌05.90.27.84.63)*. Perched atop a hill, this establishment benefits from an unobstructed view of the ocean, stretching out to the horizon. To make the most of this splendid landscape, every room has a large balcony – almost an extra room in itself! – where you can relax and contemplate the sea from afar. The simply-decorated rooms are very well-maintained and perfect for those seeking decent accommodations that don't cost a fortune. Good value for the money.

Anse des Cayes

The **Nid d'Aigle** *(400 F; ≈; 97133, ☎05.90.27.75.20)* is a pleasant, friendly and inexpensive place on the hill overhanging Anse des Cayes. It offers simple rooms bereft of any superfluous luxury. Only the bare essentials are provided: a bed, a small bathroom and a cupboard. The establishment is clean, however, and has an exceptional location with a stunning view. Moreover, the large terrain allows guests to fully enjoy this landscape.

The **Yuana** *(1,200 F; ≈, ≡, ⊛, K; 97133, ☎05.90.27.80.84, ⇌05.90.27.78.45)* is a lovely establishment facing the ocean stretching out into the distance. Perched atop a hill, it consists of several bungalows housing comfortable rooms, charmingly appointed with pleasing pastel-coloured rattan furniture.

The villas of the **Manapany** *(2,300 F bkfst incl.; ≡, ≈, ⊛, ⊛, tv, ℜ; B.P. 114, Anse des Cayes 97133, ☎05.90.27.66.55, ⇌05.90.27.75.28)* hotel lie right at the heart of the tiny and charming cove of Anse des Cayes. The white buildings have large bay windows overlooking the sea and comfortable rooms. The hotel's garden is a lovely place to stroll and forget about your worries.

Anse des Flamands

Anse des Flamands is the last long beach on the northwestern side of the island. A few hotels have taken advantage of this beautiful and secluded natural site.

At the very end of Flamands Bay stand the bungalows of the **Auberge de la Petite Anse** *(700F; ≈, K; B.P. 153, 97133, ☎05.90.27.64.89, ≈05.90.27.83.09)*, which seem to cling to the cliff's edge. The sixteen charming bungalows are not flashy, but offer all the comforts (each has a kitchenette) and are set on pleasant grounds.

The **Baie des Anges** *(1300F; ≈, ≈, ℛ, K; B.P. 162, 97133, ☎05.90.27.63.61, ≈05.90.27.83.44)* hotel is set in a very lovely sky-blue, wooden-slat building. The living quarters, all of which come with private terrace, have splendid ocean views and large rooms decorated with tropical-coloured rattan furnishings. Moreover, the establishment has a lovely swimming pool out on the cliffside. The idyllic site is far from the bustle, surrounded by nothing but the ocean which stretches as far as the eye can see.

 The beautiful buildings of the **St-Barth Isle de France** *(2,720 F bkfst incl.; B.P. 612, Anse des Flamands 97098, ☎05.90.27.61.81, ≈05.90.27.86.83)* lie nearby. The main house was built right at the edge of the shimmering sea; to take full advantage of this stunning setting, it has a large terrace overlooking the idyllic landscape. The guest rooms are not located in this building, but in villas scattered throughout the large property. Even though they were not built right by the sea, special touches like their beautiful furnishings, lovely draperies and large bay windows create a very pleasant ambience nonetheless.

✗ RESTAURANTS

Saint Barts has many excellent gourmet restaurants, friendly bistros specializing in French and Creole food, and little cafes serving sandwiches and ice cream. There is food to satisfy every taste, so you have nothing to worry when it comes to dining.

SAINT BARTS

Gustavia

You won't have any trouble finding a good restaurant in Gustavia, especially at lunch time, when the terraces open up and good daily specials top the menus.

On Rue du Roi Oscar II, you'll find the **Rôtisserie-Boulangerie** *($; ☎05.90.27.66.36)* where you can stock up on bread and deli foods for a picnic. You'll find sandwiches of all kinds, roast chicken, delicious pastries and juices; if you feel like spoiling yourself, there are also Fauchon products, imported from France, to choose from.

La Petite Colombe *($; Rue Lafayette, ☎05.90.27.93.13)* offers a good selection of Viennese bread and buns, pastries and sandwiches, making it an ideal place for breakfast or lunch.

Le Select *($-$$; Rue de la France)* is the perfect spot if you're craving a burger and fries. These can be enjoyed in the outdoor dining area, set in a garden giving onto the street. The place is not among the most enchanting in Gustavia, but it does have a friendly atmosphere.

Visitors will find many establishments near the port in which to grab a bite to eat or enjoy a good meal in a relaxed atmosphere. Among these is the **Crêperie du Port** *($$; Rue Jeanne d'Arc)*, which offers a good selection of stuffed crepes.

If you would rather partake of a simple and fresh meal, head to **La Saladerie** *($$; Rue Jeanne d'Arc)*. The menu offers no extravagant dishes, but the salads (with paper thin smoked ham or warm goat cheese) and pizzas are always good. Patrons can savour these while enjoying the bustle that reigns around the port of Gustavia all day long.

Right next door, you can't miss **L'Escale** *($$-$$$; Rue Jeanne d'Arc, ☎05.90.27.81.06)*, a very popular restaurant both at lunch and dinner. This place is a favourite because of its laid-back and friendly ambiance and its wonderful view of the port. The menu itself is hardly ground-breaking, featuring such fare as pizza cooked in a wood-burning oven and pasta au gratin. The food is good — if a little pricy.

L'Ananas *($$$; opens at noon; Rue de l'Église)*, a charming French restaurant whose terrace is all but camouflaged by vegetation, is easy to find and is ideal for a quiet meal. At lunch time, the menu lists unpretentious dishes such as salads and pizzas. In the evening, a full range of dishes is offered, and patrons will have much to choose from among a variety of fish and seafood dishes.

The **Jungle Café** *($$$; noon to midnight; Rue Jeanne d'Arc)* has the most marvellous decor, a fanciful change from the traditional seaside terraces. What better setting to savour their exotic specialties. Thai and Chinese dishes are served here for both lunch and dinner. The place is also a popular bar (see p 177).

L'Iguane *($$$; every day except Sunday; Rue de la République, ☎05.90.27.88.46)* is the place for Japanese dining in Gustavia. The menu here consists primarily of sushi and sashimi, most welcome and delicious culinary experiences on a hot day.

The main reason to go to the **Repaire des Rebelles et des Émigrés** *($$$; Rue de la République, ☎05.90.27.72.48)* is its beautiful dining room, opening on the marina and fitted out with wooden furniture and lush green plants; it exudes a subdued ambience of luxurious holidays at the beach. The ambience is perfect for lunch, when clients can enjoy watching the bustle in the streets. The place is just as pleasant in the evening, when the menu displays consistently delicious fish and seafood dishes in addition to its lunch-time fare. Breakfast is also served here.

The menu at the **Paradiso** *($$$-$$$$; lunch and dinner; closed Sat and Sun; Rue Oscar II)* reads thus: "*This menu changes with the deliveries, the catch of the day and the boss's mood*" – a guarantee that the food is always perfectly fresh. A few dishes appear regularly on the menu, such as the succulent and delightfully unique sea bream medallions in Creole sauce or rock lobster medallions with lentils. The boss, for his part, ensures that service is always attentive.

For many years a highly reputed restaurant in Gustavia, **Au Port** *($$$-$$$$; Mon to Sat 7pm; Rue du Centenaire, ☎05.90.27.62.36)* will delight diners as much with its charming dining room as with its dishes, which are always succulent. The menu is bound to give you a difficult time choosing between its French specialties (red snapper with ginger) and Creole dishes (goat *massalé*), which are equally delectable.

Outside of downtown Gustavia, you can try the restaurant of the **Carl Gustaf** *($$$$; open for lunch and supper; Rue des Normands, ☎05.90.27.82.83)* hotel, which serves elaborate dishes prepared with finesse. The chef combines French culinary techniques and regional ingredients, particularly those from the sea. While dining, guests can enjoy an unparalleled view from the magnificent terrace overlooking the sea and marina.

Saint-Jean

In the Villa Créole, at the centre of Saint-Jean, you'll find the **Rôtisserie-Boulangerie** *(70 F; Villa Créole, ☎05.90.27.73.46)*, a specialized grocer. Like its counterpart in Gustavia, it sells sandwiches and roast chicken.

In the heart of the Villa Créole, **La Créole** *($$; Villa Créole)* is a good spot for lunch, when a good and reasonably priced daily special (veal kidney with mustard sauce for 60F or tuna steak for 65F) is offered. If this does not appeal to you, note that *à-la-carte* dishes, including delicious salads, are available.

Not far from the Villa Créole, **Le Pélican** *($$$; open for lunch and supper; Saint-Jean, ☎05.90.27.64.64)* is advantageously situated on the waterfront. This no doubt explains why companies offering island tours bring their customers here for lunch. The place gets quite busy, and this popularity does have its disadvantages: come at lunchtime and you'll invariably get stuck inside, since the terrace overlooking Baie de Saint-Jean is always packed. The acclaim of this eatery is also due to its menu, which includes tasty dishes like mussels, chicken with mustard sauce and crab salad.

One of the best restaurants in Saint Barts is unquestionably the **Adam Vincent** *($$$-$$$$; ☎05.90.27.93.22)*. A veritable feast for the taste buds, each dish is inventively prepared. Whether you opt for the 190 F menu (grilled filet of red snapper with herbs) or decide to splurge for the one at 240 F (rock lobster medallions with orange butter), you are sure to be delighted. Diners will also enjoy the elegant dining room overlooking the vast expanse of ocean – an enchanting setting that complements an excellent meal. Soft music rounds off this wonderful romantic experience.

Deep in the country and thus far from the bustling cities, the restaurant of the **Hostellerie des 3 Forces** *($$$; past Lorient; watch for a sign on your right that marks the road to follow; ☎05.90.27.61.25)* enjoys a wonderfully tranquil setting. The place is perfectly secluded at nightfall, except for the few souls who have ventured off the tourist-beaten path. Here, you can savour dishes that, according to the owner, have not changed over the last 15 years. Every one of them is, of course, among the classics of French cuisine, notably the *magret de canard* (breast of duck) and the brochette of fish that, while not innovative, are always good.

At the **Eden Rock** *($$$-$$$$; lunch and dinner; ☎05.90.27.72.94)*, visitors can savour fish or seafood dishes in a stylish and friendly atmosphere that is quieter than the Pélican's (see further above). The restaurant is located in a splendid, elegantly-decorated wooden building overlooking the ocean. The food is somewhat pricey, but the location is well worth the expense.

If you are looking for quality French cuisine, you must try the restaurant at the **Filao** *($$$$; open for bkfst and lunch; Saint-Jean, ☎05.90.27.64.84)* hotel at the edge of Baie de Saint-Jean. You'll be treated to fine food, all the while enjoying the beautiful panoramic view.

Grand Cul-de-Sac

Overlooking the ocean, the **West Indies Café** *($$$$; ☎05.90.27.64.80)* is located near the swimming pool of the El Sereno hotel (see p 166). In this most pleasant location, patrons can admire the ocean while enjoying lunch, or treating themselves to delicious French cuisine as the sun sets. The evening menu offers tempting dishes, such as rock lobster fricassee with vegetables and Provencale prawns; the menu varies according to supplies.

Also located right on the beach, the **Gloriette** *($$$; ☎05.90.27.75.66)* offers a few succulent Creole specialties, notably the chicken Colombo. The setting is marvellous, and the dining room's very sober decor has been designed so as to highlight the magnificent tableau of the ocean, spread out as far as the eye can see.

Le Rivage *($$-$$$; open for lunch and supper; Petit Cul-de-Sac, ☎05.90.27.82.42)* sits at the water's edge, with its windows open to the sea so that diners can enjoy the vast expanse of shimmering blue while they savour good French and Creole meals. Among the Creole dishes are the traditional *accras*, grilled fish and *boudin créole*. Not only does the food make dining here worth your while, but the friendly atmosphere and beautiful setting add a little something extra.

Anse Toiny

When you arrive at the gourmet restaurant **Le Gaïac** *($$$$; open for lunch and supper; Hôtel Le Toiny, ☎05.90.27.88.88)*, you will be welcomed into a tastefully decorated dining room, adorned with large windows looking out onto Anse Toiny. A quick survey of the menu is enough to make you hungry. How to choose between such a vast selection of dishes, each more tempting than the last, like the large rock lobster coated with gingerbread or the *poêlée de Saint-Jacques aux échalotes et aux aubergines vinaigrées* (panfried scallops with shallots and eggplant). The meal will live up to your expectations and you'll leave with fond memories of your evening at Le Gaïac.

Located right in the vicinity of Anse de Grande Saline, the **Tamarin** *($$$; lunch; Salines, ☎05.90.27.72.12)* is a perfectly charming little restaurant in which to have lunch. Surrounded by a thousand and one plants, its terrace is delightfully shaded; it is the ideal spot to enjoy salmon carpaccio or steak tartare. More copious dishes are available on Friday, Saturday and Sunday nights.

Colombier

A lovely bakery-cake shop, the **Petite Colombe** *($;* ☎*05.90.27.95.27)* makes good sandwiches which can be enjoyed at one of the plastic tables on the eatery's miniscule terrace. Breakfast is also served here.

The restaurant in the hotel **François Plantation** *($$$$; evenings only;* ☎*05.90.27.78.82)* has a large dining room decorated with beautiful wooden furniture, rattan chairs and large picture windows that open onto the garden, creating a warm ambience. In this refined setting, patrons are treated to carefully prepared meals, worthy of the best French kitchens.

Anse des Cayes

A meal at **Ouanalao** *($$$$; Manapany hotel,* ☎*05.90.27.66.55)* is sure to be memorable, with each dish more delicious than the last. Starters include fish tartare, and are followed by one of the delectable main dishes such as veal tenderloin with a hazelnut crust and sauce amandine, fillet of beef with coffee beans and the local fish cooked in tinfoil with pink ginger. In addition to the always-delicious food, Ouanalao boasts a beautiful seaside location.

The Manapany has another, fancier restaurant, the **Ballahou** *($$$-$$$$;* ☎*05.90.27.66.55)*, which serves fine French cuisine.

Anse des Flamands

There's nothing like a fresh lobster salad for lunch, enjoyed by the pool overlooking the ocean blue. This is the scene that awaits you at **La Langouste** *($$-$$$; Baie des Anges hotel, Flamands Beach,* ☎*05.90.27.63.61)*. Perfect for lunch, it is no less enchanting at night, when the menu is somewhat more refined, featuring always-delicious and reasonably priced French and Creole specialties.

SAINT BARTS

Case de l'Isle *($$$-$$$$; open for lunch and supper; Anse des Flamands, ☎05.90.27.81.61)* is an adorable little restaurant in the St-Barth Isle de France hotel. The menu consists of delicious, classic French dishes. If you are a fan of salads or fish you are in luck, as these figure prominently on the menu.

 # ENTERTAINMENT

During the day, things are really hopping in Saint Barts, but as soon as the sun sets and it gets dark, the energy level comes down a notch or two. Most people head out for supper, ending the day with a good meal. There are, however, a few bars and discotheques for those who want to dance or have a drink. Aside from these few night spots, you can also celebrate during the holidays when lots of activities are organized. There is something for everyone, except perhaps gamblers looking to try their luck, as there are no casinos on the island.

Gustavia

There are a few pleasant bars in town, where you can spend a pleasant evening in a relaxing setting. One such establishment is the **Sélect** *(Rue France)*, a friendly bar whose simple garden is an ideal place for a beer. On certain holiday nights, musicians play here live.

Right across the street, the **Bar de l'Oubli** *(Rue de France)* gets crowded as early as 6pm, when a young clientele starts off its evening there. The place remains full late into the night. It is an ideal place to sip a drink as night falls on Gustavia.

If you prefer somewhere with a view of the marina, try **L'Escale** *(Rue Jeanne d'Arc)*. The lively atmosphere and rhythmic music set the mood. There is also a good selection of cocktails.

For a quieter evening, opt for the piano bar at the restaurant **L'Ananas** *(Rue de l'Église)*.

You can also finish your day at the **Repaire des Rebelles et des Émigrés** *(Rue de la République)*, where you can enjoy the wonderful room looking out on the marina as well as the chic yet relaxed ambiance. There is also a pool table.

🦎 The very pleasant **Jungle Café** *(Rue Jeanne d'Arc)* is unquestionably the best place on the island for a night out. Its rattan furniture, arts and crafts from around the world and wonderfully subdued lighting make it a real tropical nightspot. Patrons can also choose to sit on the terrace overlooking the marina. The establishment is frequented by people of all ages.

The bar at the **Carl Gustav** hotel distinguishes itself by its piano bar, where guests can enjoy listening to music in a relaxing setting.

Saint-Jean

At **La Créole** you can either enjoy a simple meal at the restaurant or sip a cocktail in the casual bar. The terrace is a welcoming spot.

The **Eden Rock** is right on the beach of Saint-Jean. Visitors can therefore take full advantage of this truly fabulous spot while enjoying a drink. The place attracts a well-to-do clientele.

Located right on the edge of the beach, the bar of the hotel **Filao** *(Saint-Jean)* has a magnificent view.

Grand Cul-de-Sac

In Anse du Grand Cul-de-Sac, the relaxed ambiance of the bar at the hotel **El Sereno** makes it one of the most pleasant in which to sip a drink and contemplate the ocean.

The **Cabaret La Banane** *(reservations, ☎05.90.27.64.80)* show was once held at the La Banane hotel, but neighbours' complaints forced the hoteliers to close it down. The show, always of good quality, has since moved to the El Sereno hotel (see p 166).

SAINT BARTS

Wednesday nights, the **Guanahani** hotel's restaurant livens up, resonating with Caribbean music as a dance troupe performs here.

SHOPPING

Tax-free Saint Barts is a veritable shopper's paradise; this pastime has thus quickly become one of the most popular on the island. To better serve visitors, the island's shops are stocked with an abundance of wares of all kinds, often of good quality: jewellery, household articles, clothing, perfume, cosmetics. The majority of these shops are located in Gustavia and in Saint-Jean's shopping centres.

Stores open early in the morning (8am), and most close for lunch (between noon and 2pm), then reopen until 5pm or 6pm. They are closed on Sundays.

Gustavia

Clothing and Accessories

Beautiful garments by French and Italian designers can be purchased in chic establishments such as **Cacharel** *(Rue du Général de Gaulle)*, **Gucci** *(Rue du Bord de Mer)* and **Ralph Lauren** *(Rue Auguste Nyman)*.

For classic but relatively affordable clothes, try **Pati Séragraphie** *(Rue Schœlcher)* or **Stéphane et Bernard** *(Rue de la République)*.

Three good shops to keep in mind for lovely beach-wear and swimsuits are **Calypso** *(Rue de la République)*, **Outremer** *(Rue de la République)* and **Kanelle** *(Rue du Général de Gaulle)*. The boutique **Homme de la mer** *(Rue du Général de Gaulle)* has a fine collection of beach-wear for men.

T-shirt collectors will have a field day in Gustavia. A few shops stand out from the others with their selection of tropical T-shirts: **Couleurs des Îles** *(Rue du Général de Gaulle)* and **Hookipa** *(Rue du Bord de Mer)*.

Visitors will notice people throughout the island wearing great T-shirts with the following logo: **"St. Barth West French Indies"**; these can be found in the shop of the same name on Rue de la République.

The trendiest T-shirts are probably those sold at **St. Barth d'Abord** *(Quai de la République)*. They are all adorned with a flag that once graced the ships of the island's inhabitants.

Vacationers are sure to find something at **Linnz'e** *(Rue de la France)*, which has a lovely collection of swimsuits, bikinis and sarongs.

Clémentine et Julien *(Rue du Roi Oscar II)* carries very attractive garments for children of all ages, from newborns to 14-year-olds. Pyjamas, pants, skirts, hats — everything for the little ones.

Souvenirs and Gifts

Visitors can purchase posters from **Martine Cotten** *(Rue de la République)*, who paints very charming and romantic Caribbean scenes.

For a souvenir, a statuette or some kind of decorative object, both **La Quichenotte** *(Rue du Centenaire)* and **Papayo** *(Rue du Général de Gaulle)* have beautiful collections of Creole arts and crafts.

Sailing buffs will find their heart's content at **Loulou's Marine** *(Rue de la France)*.

The **Petite Maison de Marie St. Barth** *(Rue du Roi Oscar II)* is just the place for those seeking lovely presents to bring home. Household articles, dishes and bath towels as well as high-quality clothing printed with the boutique's attractive logos are just some of the items to be found here.

Jewellery

Visitors shopping for a choice bracelet, necklace or earrings can take a look at the magnificent collections at **Carat** *(Rue de la*

SAINT BARTS

République), **Fabienne Miot** *(Rue de la République)*, **Cartier** *(Rue de la République)*, **Little Switzerland** *(Rue de France)* and **Oro de Sol** *(Rue de la République)*, especially if cost is not an issue. You can also let yourself be tempted by curios or Baccarat, Daum and Lalique crystal.

Those whose budgets or tastes are more inclined toward seashell or mother-of-pearl jewellery can visit the **Shell Shop** *(Rue du Général de Gaulle)*.

Perfumes and Cosmetics

Visitors will find a wide range of beauty products as well as French and American perfumes in the **Chamade** *(Rue de la République)* and **Privilège** *(Rue de la République)* boutiques.

Soap, sun lotion, after-sun moisturizer, herbal shampoo and many other body lotions: you'll find all this and more at **Gustavia Santé Beauté** *(Rue du Bord de l'Eau)*.

Cigars, Wine and Spirits

To stock up on cigars, fine wines and spirits, three shops should be kept in mind: **Smoke and Booze** *(Rue du Général de Gaulle)*, **La Cave** *(Quai de la République)* and, for Cuban or Dominican cigars, the **Comptoir du Cigare** *(Rue du Général de Gaulle)*.

Saint-Jean

Clothing and Accessories

Shoppers looking for high-quality bathing suits and beach-wear will have much to choose from at the **Black Swan** *(Villa Créole)* boutique.

Right next door, **Surf Shop** *(Villa Créole)* also offers terrific swimsuits with more sporty cuts.

Biba *(Saint-Jean shopping centre)* is yet another fine store that sells swimsuits.

For casual, classically-tailored clothes, **Stéphane et Bernard** *(La Savane, facing the airport)* is a must.

Holiday-makers are sure to find attractive apparel, perfect for the island's climate, at **Morgan** *(Villa Saint-Jean)*.

Jewellery

Kornerupine *(Villa Créole)* also offers an attractive selection of seashell, silver and gold jewellery.

Groceries

You can buy most provisions at the **Match** supermarket across from the airport.

Souvenirs and Gifts

Saint Barts T-shirts and beauty products, as well as a host of other quality products made on the island, can be found at **Made in Saint-Barth** *(Saint-Jean shopping centre)*.

Lorient

Perfume and Cosmetics

If you are looking for products more typical of Saint Barts, **La Ligne de Saint-Barth** *(Route de Saline)* is an absolute must. They sell a line of beauty products made right on the premises from natural ingredients.

Groceries

There are two adjacent grocery stores in Lorient, the **Mini Mart** and **Jojo Supermarket**, both of which offer a good selection.

ENGLISH-FRENCH GLOSSARY

GREETINGS

Hi (casual)	*Salut*
How are you?	*Comment ça va?*
I'm fine	*Ça va bien*
Hello (during the day)	*Bonjour*
Good evening/night	*Bonsoir*
Goodbye, See you later	*Bonjour, Au revoir, à la prochaine*
Yes	*Oui*
No	*Non*
Maybe	*Peut-être*
Please	*S'il vous plaît*
Thank you	*Merci*
You're welcome	*De rien, Bienvenue*
Excuse me	*Excusez-moi*
I am a tourist.	*Je suis touriste*
I am American (m/f)	*Je suis Américain(e)*
I am Canadian (m/f)	*Je suis Canadien(ne)*
I am British	*Je suis Britannique*
I am German (m/f)	*Je suis Allemand(e)*
I am Italian (male/female)	*Je suis Italien(ne)*
I am Belgian	*Je suis Belge*
I am Swiss	*Je suis Suisse*
I am sorry, I don't speak French	*Je suis désolé(e), je ne parle pas français*
Do you speak English?	*Parlez-vous anglais ?*
Slower, please.	*Plus lentement, s'il vous plaît.*
What is your name?	*Quel est votre nom?*
My name is...	*Je m'appelle...*
spouse (m/f)	*époux(se)*
brother, sister	*frère, soeur*
friend (m/f)	*ami(e)*
son, boy	*garçon*
daughter, girl	*fille*
father	*père*
mother	*mère*
single (m/f)	*celibataire*
married (m/f)	*marié(e)*
divorced (m/f)	*divorcé(e)*
widower/widow	*veuf(ve)*

DIRECTIONS

Is there a tourism office near here?	*Est-ce qu'il y a un bureau de tourisme près d'ici?*
There is no...	*Il n'y a pas de...,*
Where is...?	*Où est le/la ... ?*

straight ahead	*tout droit*
to the right	*à droite*
to the left	*à gauche*
beside	*à côté de*
near	*près de*
here	*ici*
there, over there	*là, là-bas*
into, inside	*à l'intérieur*
outside	*à l'extérieur*
far from	*loin de*
between	*entre*
in front of	*devant*
behind	*derrière*

GETTING AROUND

airport	*aéroport*
on time	*à l'heure*
late	*en retard*
cancelled	*annulé*
plane	*l'avion*
car	*la voiture*
train	*le train*
boat	*le bateau*
bicycle	*la bicyclette, le vélo*
bus	*l'autobus*
train station	*la gare*
bus stop	*un arrêt d'autobus*
The bus stop, please	*l'arrêt, s'il vous plaît*
street	*rue*
avenue	*avenue*
road	*route, chemin*
highway	*autoroute*
rural route	*rang*
path, trail	*sentier*
corner	*coin*
neighbourhood	*quartier*
square	*place*
tourist office	*bureau de tourisme*
bridge	*pont*
building	*immeuble*
safe	*sécuritaire*
fast	*rapide*
baggage	*bagages*
schedule	*horaire*
one way ticket	*aller simple*
return ticket	*aller retour*
arrival	*arrivée*
return	*retour*
departure	*départ*

north	*nord*
south	*sud*
east	*est*
west	*ouest*

CARS

for rent	*à louer*
a stop	*un arrêt*
highway	*autoroute*
danger, be careful	*attention*
no passing	*défense de doubler*
no parking	*stationnement interdit*
no exit	*impasse*
stop! (an order)	*arrêtez!*
parking	*stationnement*
pedestrians	*piétons*
gas	*essence*
slow down	*ralentir*
traffic light	*feu de circulation*
service station	*station-service*
speed limit	*limite de vitesse*

MONEY

bank	*banque*
credit union	*caisse populaire*
exchange	*change*
money	*argent*
I don't have any money	*je n'ai pas d'argent*
credit card	*carte de crédit*
traveller's cheques	*chèques de voyage*
The bill please	*l'addition, s'il vous plaît*
receipt	*reçu*

ACCOMMODATION

inn	*auberge*
youth hostel	*auberge de jeunesse*
bed and breakfast	*gîte*
hot water	*eau chaude*
air conditioning	*climatisation*
accommodation	*logement, hébergement*
elevator	*ascenseur*
bathroom	*toilettes, salle de bain*
bed	*lit*
breakfast	*déjeuner*
manager, owner	*gérant, propriétaire*
bedroom	*chambre*
pool	*piscine*
floor (first, second...)	*étage*
main floor	*rez-de-chaussée*

high season	*haute saison*
off season	*basse saison*
fan	*ventilateur*

SHOPPING

open	*ouvert(e)*
closed	*fermé(e)*
How much is this?	*C'est combien?*
I would like...	*Je voudrais...*
I need...	*J'ai besoin de...*
a store	*un magasin*
a department store	*un magasin à rayons*
the market	*le marché*
salesperson (m/f)	*vendeur(se)*
the customer (m/f)	*le / la client(e)*
to buy	*acheter*
to sell	*vendre*
t-shirt	*un t-shirt*
skirt	*une jupe*
shirt	*une chemise*
jeans	*un jeans*
pants	*des pantalons*
jacket	*un blouson*
blouse	*une blouse*
shoes	*des souliers*
sandals	*des sandales*
hat	*un chapeau*
eyeglasses	*des lunettes*
handbag	*un sac*
gifts	*cadeaux*
local crafts	*artisanat local*
sun protection products	*crèmes solaires*
cosmetics and perfumes	*cosmétiques et parfums*
camera	*appareil photo*
photographic film	*pellicule*
records, cassettes	*disques, cassettes*
newspapers	*journaux*
magazines	*revues, magazines*
batteries	*piles*
watches	*montres*
jewellery	*bijouterie*
gold	*or*
silver	*argent*
precious stones	*pierres précieuses*
fabric	*tissu*
wool	*laine*
cotton	*coton*
leather	*cuir*

MISCELLANEOUS

new	*nouveau*
old	*vieux*
expensive	*cher, dispendieux*
inexpensive	*pas cher*
pretty	*joli*
beautiful	*beau*
ugly	*laid(e)*
big, tall (person)	*grand(e)*
small, short (person)	*petit(e)*
short (length)	*court(e)*
low	*bas(se)*
wide	*large*
narrow	*étroit(e)*
dark	*foncé*
light (colour)	*clair*
fat (person)	*gros(se)*
slim, skinny (person)	*mince*
a little	*peu*
a lot	*beaucoup*
something	*quelque chose*
nothing	*rien*
good	*bon*
bad	*mauvais*
more	*plus*
less	*moins*
do not touch	*ne pas toucher*
quickly	*vite*
slowly	*lentement*
big	*grand*
small	*petit*
hot	*chaud*
cold	*froid*
I am ill	*je suis malade*
pharmacy, drugstore	*pharmacie*
I am hungry	*j'ai faim*
I am thirsty	*j'ai soif*
What is this?	*Qu'est-ce que c'est?*
Where?	*Où?*
fixed price menu	*table d'hôte*
order courses separately	*à la carte*

WEATHER

rain	*pluie*
clouds	*nuages*
sun	*soleil*
It is hot out	*Il fait chaud*
It is cold out	*Il fait froid*

TIME

When?	*Quand?*
What time is it?	*Quelle heure est-il?*
minute	*minute*
hour	*heure*
day	*jour*
week	*semaine*
month	*mois*
year	*année*
yesterday	*hier*
today	*aujourd'hui*
tommorrow	*demain*
morning	*le matin*
afternoon	*l'après-midi*
evening	*le soir*
night	*la nuit*
now	*maintenant*
never	*jamais*
Sunday	*dimanche*
Monday	*lundi*
Tuesday	*mardi*
Wednesday	*mercredi*
Thursday	*jeudi*
Friday	*vendredi*
Saturday	*samedi*
January	*janvier*
February	*février*
March	*mars*
April	*avril*
May	*mai*
June	*juin*
July	*juillet*
August	*août*
September	*septembre*
October	*octobre*
November	*novembre*
December	*décembre*

COMMUNICATION

post office	*bureau de poste*
air mail	*par avion*
stamps	*timbres*
envelope	*enveloppe*
telephone book	*bottin téléphonique*
long distance call	*appel outre-mer*
collect call	*appel collecte*
fax	*télécopieur, fax*
telegram	*télégramme*
rate	*tarif*

dial the regional code	*composer le code régional*
wait for the tone	*attendre la tonalité*

ACTIVITIES

recreational swimming	*la baignade*
beach	*plage*
scuba diving	*la plongée sous-marine*
snorkelling	*la plongée-tuba*
fishing	*la pêche*
recreational sailing	*navigation de plaisance*
windsurfing	*la planche à voile*
bicycling	*faire du vélo*
mountain bike	*vélo tout-terrain (VTT)*
horseback riding	*équitation*
hiking	*la randonnée pédestre*
to walk around	*se promener*
museum or gallery	*musée*
cultural centre	*centre culturel*
cinema	*cinéma*

TOURING

river	*fleuve, rivière*
waterfalls	*chutes*
viewpoint	*belvédère*
hill	*colline*
garden	*jardin*
wildlife reserve	*réserve faunique*
peninsula	*péninsule, presqu'île*
south/north shore	*côte sud/nord*
town or city hall	*hôtel de ville*
court house	*palais de justice*
church	*église*
house	*maison*
manor	*manoir*
bridge	*pont*
basin	*bassin*
dam	*barrage*
workshop	*atelier*
historic site	*lieu historique*
train station	*gare*
stables	*écuries*
convent	*couvent*
door, archway, gate	*porte*
customs house	*douane*
locks	*écluses*
market	*marché*
canal	*canal*
channel	*chenal*
seaway	*voie maritime*

museum	*musée*
cemetery	*cimitière*
mill	*moulin*
windmill	*moulin à vent*
hospital	*Hôtel Dieu*
high school	*école secondaire*
lighthouse	*phare*
barn	*grange*
waterfall(s)	*chute(s)*
sandbank	*batture*
neighbourhood, region	*faubourg*

NUMBERS

1	*un*	22	*vingt-deux*
2	*deux*	23	*vingt-trois*
3	*trois*	24	*vingt-quatre*
4	*quatre*	25	*vingt-cinq*
5	*cinq*	26	*vingt-six*
6	*six*	27	*vingt-sept*
7	*sept*	28	*vingt-huit*
8	*huit*	29	*vingt-neuf*
9	*neuf*	30	*trente*
10	*dix*	40	*quarante*
11	*onze*	50	*cinquante*
12	*douze*	60	*soixante*
13	*treize*	70	*soixante-dix*
14	*quatorze*	80	*quatre-vingt*
15	*quinze*	90	*quatre-vingt-dix*
16	*seize*	100	*cent*
17	*dix-sept*	200	*deux cents*
18	*dix-huit*	500	*cinq cents*
19	*dix-neuf*	1,000	*mille*
20	*vingt*	10,000	*dix mille*
21	*vingt-et-un*	1,000,000	*un million*

INDEX

Accommodations (cont'd)

INDEX

INDEX

INDEX

INDEX

INDEX

Acapulco (Mexico)
Ulysses Due South guide offers a fresh look at Acapulco, the most famous Mexican resort: Acapulco Bay, its beaches, restaurants and captivating nightlife are all in there, but so are the neighbouring mountains, as well as an enlightened look at the people and history of this spot.
Marc Rigole, Claude-Victor Langlois   150 pages, 5 maps
$14.95 CAN $9.95 US   £6.99
2-89464-062-5

Belize
This tiny Central American country encompasses part of the ancient Ruta Maya and is rimmed by spectacular coral reefs. Its archaeological and natural treasures make it an explorer's paradise. Practical and cultural information will help you make the most of your vacation.
Carlos Soldevila   208 pages, 10 maps
$12.95 US
2-89464-179-6

Cancún & Cozumel (Mexico)
The entirely man-made resort of Cancún on the Yucatán Peninsula attracts visitors from the world-over. They come to enjoy a unique travelling experience with fabulous archaeological sites, the last remnants of the Mayan civilization, and the island of Cozumel, a scuba-diver's paradise, both close by.
Caroline Vien, Alain Théroux   200 pages, 20 maps
$17.95 CAN $12.95 US   £8.99
2-89464-040-4

Cartagena, 2nd edition
Here is the new edition on this colonial jewel. Declared a World Heritage Site by UNESCO, Cartagena boasts historic charm, cultural riches, luxurious hotels, beautiful beaches and the possibility of exciting excursions, all the ingredients for an extraordinary vacation.
Marc Rigole   128 pages, 10 maps
$12.95 CAN $9.95 US   £6.50
2-89464-018-8

Costa Rica
This fresh look at Costa Rica provides travellers with the most extensive choice of practical addresses, no matter what their budget while also placing special emphasis on eco-tourism, independent travel and the culture, history and natural wonders of this Central American gem.
Francis Giguère, Yves Séguin   368 pages, 35 maps
8 pages of colour photos
$27.95 CAN $19.95 US   £13.99
2-89464-144-3

Cuba, 2nd edition
Already a second edition for this unique guide to Cuba. The island's spirit is revealed, from colonial Havana, to the world-heritage site of Trinidad and to Santiago with it Afro-Cuban culture. The guide also covers the famous beaches and provides travellers with countless shortcuts and tips for independent travel in Cuba.
Carlos Soldevila   336 pages, 40 maps
8 pages of colour photos
$24.95 CAN $17.95 US   £12.99
2-89464-143-5

Dominican Republic
The most complete reference to this Caribbean hot spot: excursions, historical information, cultural details, addresses of restaurants, shops and hotels, road maps and city plans.
Pascale Couture, Benoit Prieur
250 pages, 20 maps
8 pages of colour photos
$24.95 CAN $17.95 US   £12.99
2-89464-064-1

Ecuador and the Galápagos Islands
All the major sites of this South American country are explored including extensive coverage of the capital city, Quito, but also the extraordinary Galapagos Islands. Hundreds of addresses for all budgets as well as countless useful hints for discovering this fascinating and ancient land of the Incas.
Alain Legault   300 pages, 25 maps
8 pages of colour photos
$24.95 CAN $17.95 US   £12.99
2-89464-059-5

El Salvador
This guide provides everything the traveller needs to discover this fascinating Central American country: explanation of cultural and political contexts, advice on how to travel in the area, descriptions of the various attractions, detailed lists of accommodation, restaurants, entertainment.
Eric Hamovitch   152 pages, 7 maps
$22.95 CAN $14.95 US   £11.50
2-921444-89-5

Guatemala
Historic peace talks have once again allowed tourism to develop in Guatemala, providing a glimpse at a country whose native traditions are so strong and omnipresent.
Carlos Soldevila, Denis Faubert   336 pages, 30 maps
$24.95 CAN $17.95 US   £12.99
2-89464-175-3

Honduras, 2nd edition

The prospects for tourism in Honduras are among the brightest – promising travellers a first-rate vacation, whether they are in search of spectacular deserted beaches, fascinating archaeological sites or supreme diving locations. This guide offers numerous suggestions for outdoor adventure plus practical tips and information on everything from A to Z.

Eric Hamovitch   224 pages, 20 maps
$24.95 CAN $17.95 US   £12.99
2-89464-132-X

Nicaragua

Once a headline-maker the world over, Nicaragua is more often featured in the "Travel" section these days. Besides the capital city of Managua and the popular resort of Montelimar, this guide traverses the whole country, discovering the touching cities of León and Granada, among other places, along the way.

Carol Wood   224 pages, 15 maps
$24.95 CAN $16.95 US   £11.50
2-89464-034-X

Panamá, 2nd edition

Famous for its impressive canal, Panamá offers magnificent beaches on two different oceans, nestled in a diverse ethnic and cultural environment. This guide will help the traveller discover an infinite variety of landscapes, with unequalled flora and fauna.

Marc Rigole, Claude-Victor Langlois   208 pages, 16 maps
8 pages of colour photos
$24.95 CAN $16.95 US   £11.50
2-89464-005-6

Peru

Ulysses reveals the stunning scenery of this varied land: the Inca Trail and the ancient Inca city of Macchu Pichu, the depths of the Amazon rainforest, the high reaches of the Cordillera Blanca, modern and bustling Lima and beautiful Arequipa. An insightful portrait and a thorough how-to section round out the guide.

Alain Legault   352 pages, 60 maps
8 pages of colour photos
$17.95 US
2-89464-122-2

Puerto Vallarta (Mexico)

What began as a tiny fishing village nestled between sea and mountains has blossomed into one of the Mexican Riviera's most splendid resorts. This guide reveals the splendour of Puerto Vallarta, from its luxuriant flora to its quaint tile-roofed houses and countless excellent restaurants.

Richard Bizier, Roch Nadeau   160 pages, 5 maps
$14.95 CAN $9.95 US   £6.50
2-89464-039-0

TRAVEL BETTER... TRAVEL THE NET

Visit our web site
to travel better...
to discover, to explore
and to enjoy more

www.ulysses.ca

Catalogue

Talk to us

Order

Distributors

History

Internet
Travel

ORDER FORM

ULYSSES TRAVEL GUIDES

☐ Atlantic Canada	$24.95 CAN $17.95 US	☐ Lisbon	$18.95 CAN $13.95 US
☐ Bahamas	$24.95 CAN $17.95 US	☐ Louisiana	$29.95 CAN $21.95 US
☐ Beaches of Maine	$12.95 CAN $9.95 US	☐ Martinique	$24.95 CAN $17.95 US
☐ Bed & Breakfasts in Québec	$13.95 CAN $10.95 US	☐ Montréal	$19.95 CAN $14.95 US
☐ Belize	$16.95 CAN $12.95 US	☐ New Orleans	$17.95 CAN $12.95 US
☐ Calgary	$17.95 CAN $12.95 US	☐ New York City	$19.95 CAN $14.95 US
☐ Canada	$29.95 CAN $21.95 US	☐ Nicaragua	$24.95 CAN $16.95 US
☐ Chicago	$19.95 CAN $14.95 US	☐ Ontario	$27.95 CAN $19.95US
☐ Chile	$27.95 CAN $17.95 US	☐ Ottawa	$17.95 CAN $12.95 US
☐ Colombia	$29.95 CAN $21.95 US	☐ Panamá	$24.95 CAN $17.95 US
☐ Costa Rica	$27.95 CAN $19.95 US	☐ Peru	$27.95 CAN $19.95 US
☐ Cuba	$24.95 CAN $17.95 US	☐ Portugal	$24.95 CAN $16.95 US
☐ Dominican Republic	$24.95 CAN $17.95 US	☐ Provence - Côte d'Azur	$29.95 CAN $21.95US
☐ Ecuador and Galapagos Islands	$24.95 CAN $17.95 US	☐ Québec	$29.95 CAN $21.95 US
☐ El Salvador	$22.95 CAN $14.95 US	☐ Québec and Ontario with Via	$9.95 CAN $7.95 US
☐ Guadeloupe	$24.95 CAN $17.95 US	☐ Toronto	$18.95 CAN $13.95 US
☐ Guatemala	$24.95 CAN $17.95 US	☐ Vancouver	$17.95 CAN $12.95 US
☐ Honduras	$24.95 CAN $17.95 US	☐ Washington D.C.	$18.95 CAN $13.95 US
☐ Jamaica	$24.95 CAN $17.95 US	☐ Western Canada	$29.95 CAN $21.95 US

ULYSSES DUE SOUTH

☐ Acapulco	$14.95 CAN $9.95 US	☐ Cartagena (Colombia)	$12.95 CAN $9.95 US
☐ Belize	$16.95 CAN $12.95 US	☐ Cancun Cozumel	$17.95 CAN $12.95 US

ULYSSES DUE SOUTH

□ Puerto Vallarta . $14.95 CAN
$9.95 US

□ St. Martin and . $16.95 CAN
St. Barts $12.95 US

ULYSSES TRAVEL JOURNAL

□ Ulysses Travel Journal . . . . $9.95 CAN
(Blue, Red, Green, Yellow, Sextant) $7.95 US

ULYSSES GREEN ESCAPES

□ Cycling in France $22.95 CAN
$16.95 US

□ Cycling in Ontario $22.95 CAN
$16.95 US

□ Hiking in the . . . $19.95 CAN
Northeastern U.S. $13.95 US

□ Hiking in Québec $19.95 CAN
$13.95 US

TITLE	QUANTITY	PRICE	TOTAL

Name _____	Sub-total	
Address _____	Postage & Handling	$8.00*
_____	Sub-total	
_____		
Payment : □ Money Order □ Visa □ MasterCard	G.S.T. in Canada 7%	
Card Number _____		
Signature _____	TOTAL	

ULYSSES TRAVEL PUBLICATIONS
4176 St-Denis,
Montréal, Québec, H2W 2M5
(514) 843-9447 fax (514) 843-9448
www.ulysses.ca
* $15 for overseas orders

U.S. ORDERS: **GLOBE PEQUOT PRESS**
P.O. Box 833, 6 Business Park Road,
Old Saybrook, CT 06475-0833
1-800-243-0495 fax 1-800-820-2329
www.globe-pequot.com